Quirky Quotations

Also by Tad Tuleja

FABULOUS FALLACIES

CURIOUS CUSTOMS

MARVELOUS MONIKERS

FOREIGNISMS

THE CAT'S PAJAMAS

THE CATALOG OF LOST BOOKS

AMERICAN HISTORY IN 100 NUTSHELLS

Quirky Quotations

More Than 500

Fascinating,

Quotable Comments

and the Stories

Behind Them

Tad Tuleja

A Stonesong Press Book

Harmony Books
New York

For my mother
Elizabeth Stokes Tuleja
who at seventy
has the sparkle of seventeen

Published by Harmony Books, a division of Crown Publishers, Inc., 201 East 50th Street, New York, New York 10022. Member of the Crown Publishing Group.

HARMONY and colophon are trademarks of Crown Publishers, Inc.

Manufactured in the United States of America

A Stonesong Press Book

Library of Congress Cataloging-in-Publication Data
Tuleja, Tad
Quirky quotations : more than 500 fascinating,
quotable comments and the stories behind them / by Tad Tuleja.—1st ed.
p.   cm.
"A Stonesong Press book."
1. Quotations.   I. Title.
PN6081.T85   1992
082—dc20   92-2501
                                            CIP

ISBN 0-517-58560-X
10   9   8   7   6   5   4   3   2   1

First Edition

Contents

11

...And Other Cuts
(Insults)
121

12

Predictions That Time Forgot
(Missed Takes)
136

13

Second Drafts
(Updated Quotes)
146

14

The Fab Four
(A Quartet of Quipsters)
159

15

What's It All About, Alfie?
(Life)
169

16

The End
(Death and Last Words)
180

Introduction

Every collection reveals both the prejudices of its time and the slant of its owner's obsessions. A collection of sayings is no exception. Back in the 1790s, when a university education meant a classical education, D. E. Macdonnel's *Dictionary of Quotations* featured selections "chiefly from Latin and French," that is, from the epigrams of Martial to those of Montaigne. In John Bartlett's day, aphorism droppers leaned heavily on the Bible and the Bard: Thus his 1855 book of memorable mouthfuls contained generous helpings from the evangelists and *King Lear*. A century later, when the editors of the *Oxford Dictionary of Quotations* made their cuts, the literary taste of their generation was revealed. Of the top ten authors represented, fully half of them—Browning, Byron, Shelley, Tennyson, and Wordsworth—came from the previous century's established poetic pantheon.

In our relatively faithless and increasingly specialized age, quotation chrestomathies tend toward cynicism and narrow, even partisan, utility. The superb collections of Bartlett, Burton Stevenson, and Bennett Cerf are still making the rounds, but smaller vade mecums are gradually edging them out. Volumes with titles such as *The Book of Insults* and *The Toastmaster's Companion* and *War Words* provide brief, useful snippets "for every occasion" to those who—unlike Bartlett's audience—do not have the time or interest to read the originals. Many of these books display intelligence as well as wit, but the distillation is sometimes tendentious as well as intemperate. Where Oxford gave all of Hamlet's best-remembered soliloquy, today we're likely to find merely "There's the rub"—in a book called *Bon Mots for the Masseur*.

To define what is going on here, we can use a fashionable term that, like the monster movies' servant Igor, is as helpful as it is unattractive. We are witnessing a process of "decontextualization" through which comments on the human condition are snatched from their biographical, social, and philosophical environments and plopped down for the browser's attention on a tabula rasa, like fugitive diadems from a New Critic's crown. It is hardly surprising that in this shopper's paradise of thoughts the preferred vendors include those masters of the disembodied one-liner, George Bernard Shaw, H. L. Mencken, and Oscar Wilde.

Now, I love a Shavian jab as well as the next person and confess that if doomed to spend eternity with another writer I would want to choose between this sniggering triad and Mr. Dooley. However, in *Quirky Quotations* I have set myself a different goal—not the presentation of remarkable comments in and of themselves but their (here's Igor again) "recontextualization" into their environments. If quotation books can be seen as verbal banquets, this one's laid for diners, not noshers. For most of the hundreds of treats on this table, I give some idea of where they came from and how they got here. Reading it, you can look a gift Horace in the mouth.

A word on the logic behind my selections. I've entitled the collection *Quirky Quotations* because, as a child of postmodernism, I'm as "tweaked" in my views of life as Bartlett was sober. Many of the quotes here are in some way a little off-the-wall. They betray cynicism in a sentimental, rather than merely snappish, manner; they glisten with paradox or irony; they come trailing clouds of strange story; or they simply suggest, as the best epigrams of Wilde (or for that matter Montaigne) suggest, that at the heart of things tears and laughter are the same response. A good epigram doesn't drench you with the water of wisdom; it's a splash in the face, part taunt, part blessing. So what I've tried for is less portent, more punch.

The range of authors is also a little quirky. Very little Wilde, Mencken, or Shaw. Even less from Ecclesiastes and the Bard. Nothing from La Rochefoucauld. This neglect of the old standbys is intentional. While there are plenty of familiar lines in this volume, I've tried to stick, for the most part, to the road less traveled by and to seek out flowers that are not already in most gardens. To cite only the most obvious example, chapter 14 includes selections from my Fab Four authors. Not Shakespeare, Shaw, Twain, and Dr. Johnson, but Sydney Smith, Elbert Hubbard, Ambrose Bierce, and Dorothy Parker. Such second-magnitude stars are on center stage throughout the book.

Quirky Quotations came together during one of the most hectic and challenging summers of my life. For tolerating my schedule and preserving my perspective, my wife, Andrée, and our daughter, India, have earned the heartfelt gratitude of a lucky guy. My thanks as well to Jeanne and Claude, for providing us gypsies a warm abode as we moved the teepee. To my father, a belated thanks for the *Penguin Dictionary of Quotations,* which he gave me a decade ago with the hopeful wish "*que ton éducation ne laisse rien à désirer.*" My debt to him, and to the woman who has borne the two of us for almost fifty years, cannot be paid but in due honor and deep affection.

T.F.T.
Austin, Texas

Nothing

that can be

said

is so absurd

that some

philosopher

has not

already said it.

—*Cicero*

chapter 1

The

Most

High

God and Religion

THE CENTER OF THINGS

At the door of the ancient Greek philosopher Empedocles (c. 490–430 B.C.) is laid one of the most sublime metaphors for God ever recorded. Popular in the Middle Ages both within and outside of scholastic cells, it suggested the vastness of divinity through a mystical geometry: "**God is a circle whose center is everywhere and whose circumference is nowhere.**" A modern deconstructionist could probably pick that apart pretty well. I prefer to go along with St. Bonaventure and nod approvingly.

One of the more versatile Presocratics, Empedocles proposed the classical Greek division of nature into the four elements (earth, air, fire, and water), spoke of love and strife as twin agents of change, and also was a fair hand at medicine. After successfully combating a plague on Sicily (only you-know-who knows how), he evidently declared himself divine, and to convince people that the other gods were calling him home, jumped into the crater of the volcano Mount Etna. With this *beau laid geste* medieval scholars were less impressed.

HEAVEN CAN WAIT

In the eighth book of his *Confessions,* St. Augustine acknowledges the tenacity of lust by recalling an ironic prayer of his youth: "**Give me chastity and self-control—but not yet.**" Cynics like to quote this passage as proof that Augustine was a hypocritical roué. That's a simplistic reading. Augustine's admission comes as a dramatic prelude to the description of his spiritual conversion, and in context it is anything but hypocritical. The chapter begins with a vivid discussion of his pre-conversion self-delusion. It ends with him acknowledging that his spirit "feared like death the cessation of that habit of which in fact it was dying." The "not yet" quote comes in between, as a reflection (not without humor) of his spiritual agony. You might not buy Augustine's belief that carnality and spirituality are mutually exclusive, but it's impossible, after reading this passage, to doubt his integrity.

GOOD KING HENRY

In France throughout the latter half of the sixteenth century, rival aristocrats slaughtered one another in the name of religion. Political jealousies informed their zeal, but theological differences were superficially important enough to dub the conflicts the Wars of Religion. The most famous slaughter happened on St. Bartholomew's Day in August 1572, when the queen dowager, Catherine de Médicis, engineered the murder of Protestants who had come to Paris to see their champion, Henry of Navarre, marry Catherine's daughter, Margaret of Valois. This attempt at denominational conciliation went badly awry: Catherine spared her new son-in-law but eliminated thirteen thousand of his fellow believers, then forced him to convert to the Roman faith.

The first of two conversions that Henry adopted, it lasted only a little beyond the wedding, when he resumed control of the Protestant armies. A permanent conversion came twenty years later, occasioning his most often quoted line. In 1589 he had acceded to the French throne, as Henry IV, first of the Bourbon line. Four years later, in order to make his rule acceptable to the powerful and intransigent Catholic League, he put away the faith of his childhood forever, explaining, "**Paris is worth a mass.**" Seldom has nationalism been more richly misted with frankincense.

Henry proved so popular and effective a monarch that he is thought of as having created the nation of France. *Le bon roi Henri,* or Good King Henry, is how the history books describe him. He later established freedom of worship by the Edict of Nantes (1598); built roads, canals, and new industries; promoted foreign trade; and sent Samuel de Champlain to North America. He lasted until the spring of 1610, when he was assassinated by a Catholic fanatic, François Ravaillac.

WOULD YOU BUY A USED CAR FROM THIS GUY?

In the Western tradition, the devil goes by many names, among them Satan, Beelzebub, Mephistopheles, the Archfiend, Old Scratch, Old Nick, the Arch-Imposter, and the Prince of Darkness. By whatever name, the character not only symbolizes evil in the abstract but also is a folkloric personage whose hand may be seen in all the specific evils of human history, from Eve's supposed foul-up with the apple to the latest war. Medieval Europe depicted the figure as supernaturally ugly, horned, and tailed. But as the Eden story indicates, the devil's peculiar skill is deception, and that skill makes him a formidable adversary. If you were offered a shot at lust, avarice, or pride by some sulfur-breathing creature out of Bosch, you'd probably look before leaping. That's why the devil, when he tempts, comes smart and smiling.

The poets have been saying this for centuries. In *King Lear* we find, "**The prince of darkness is a gentleman.**" Shelley echoes the thought and in his ballad "The Devil's Walk" describes how Beelzebub, "**his sweet person adorning, put on his Sunday clothes.**" Elizabeth Barrett Browning, in "Aurora Leigh," claims "**The devil's most devilish when respectable.**" In our own time, Bob Dylan sings dolefully, "**You know that sometimes Satan, he comes as a man of peace.**" Since "Man of Peace" is one of the epithets of Jesus Christ, you can see how far the Imposter is willing to go.

THE WORLD, THE FLESH, AND THE DEVIL

With the possible exception of the Mormons, whose history of polygamy makes them ideal targets for the prurient, the New England Puritans have probably been subjected to more witty abuse than any other religious group in America. It's fruitless for historians to point out that the stiff-necked, life-hating Puritan father was largely a figment of the nineteenth-century imagination, that Puritan theology demanded its adherents delight in God's physical world, that premarital "bundling" was a not uncommon practice among these supposedly frigid people, and that Hester Prynne was not the only New England maiden who understood what the good Lord gave us bodies for. The stereotype says the Puritan despised the world, and it's the stereotype, not the reality, that people want.

Injustice aside, the mudslinging has been amusing: Speaking of the Bay Colony settlers' English forebears, Thomas Macaulay set the tone in this dismissive picture: **"The Puritan hated bear-baiting, not because it gave pain to the bear, but because it gave pleasure to the spectators."** Echoing this view with regard to his own ancestors, Cleveland Amory claimed that the New England conscience **"does not stop you from doing what you shouldn't. It just stops you from enjoying it."** But the first prize for Pilgrimbaiting goes to H. L. Mencken. In his 1924 book *Prejudices,* he defined Puritanism as **"the haunting fear that someone, somewhere, might be happy."**

THREE PERSONS OF THE BLESSED TRIANGLE

Charles-Louis de Secondat, Baron de La Brède et de Montesquieu, was a French philosopher, jurist, and historian whose most famous book, *The Spirit of the Laws* (1748), profoundly influenced our Founding Fathers' notions of government: it brilliantly defined the principle of checks and balances. A comparative study of despotism, monarchy, and republicanism, *The Spirit of the Laws* was Montesquieu's masterpiece, finished only seven years before his death. In his own time he was just as well known for his first book, the wittily discursive satire *Persian Letters* (1721), in which a pair of exotics named Rica and Usbek comment trenchantly on French manners and institutions.

In the fifty-ninth of these letters, supposedly written at Paris on the fourteenth of "the moon of Saphar," 1714, Rica comments on the human propensity to "judge things by applying them secretly to ourselves"—that is, by making ourselves the measure of value. This is especially the case, he observes, with regard to deities. Men so consistently make themselves the "model for providence" that African gods are predictably black, while among people where pendulous breasts are a sign of beauty, the goddess of love has "breasts that hang to her thighs." It is well said, Rica concludes, supposedly quoting an old adage, **"If triangles created a god, they would make him three-sided."** Given the suspicion of organized religion shared by Montesquieu and his fellow philosophes, it seems likely that this is a subtle jab at the Christian Trinity.

NOTICING THE LITTLE THINGS

William Blake's mystical, almost pantheistic faith enabled him to paint a justly famous description of "childlike" vision. In *Auguries of Innocence,* he celebrates children's uncontaminated, or "unfallen," mode of apprehension. It is your delight while young, he writes,

> **To see a World in a Grain of Sand,**
> **And Heaven in a Wild Flower,**
> **Hold Infinity in the palm of your hand,**
> **And Eternity in an hour.**

Blake's contemporary, the German poet Friedrich Hölderlin, shared his faith in the epiphanic potential of tiny facts and chose for his motto a Latin catchphrase Blake would have admired: ***Maximo in minimo,*** or "The greatest in the least."

Blake and Hölderlin lived within—or rather, helped to generate—that marvelous efflorescence of naturist passion that became known, after the fact, as the Romantic movement. Flowers especially served that movement as symbolic coin of the realm: The poet Novalis's ***blaue***

Blume, or "blue flower," for example, was a universal symbol among his German contemporaries for Romantic longing. It's not odd to find them seizing on natural particulars to prove Blake's belief "**Everything that lives is Holy.**" It's a little odder, and quite affecting, to find this sensibility in a modern writer, yet it's clearly expressed by Alice Walker in *The Color Purple:* "**I think it pisses God off if you walk by the color purple in a field somewhere and don't notice it.**" Both the vulgarity and the reverence would have warmed Blake's heart.

YOU CALL *THAT* AN ACT OF CONTRITION?

The Supreme Being, we are told by the Judeo-Christian tradition, is a God both of justice and of compassion—yet in what proportion these two facets are mixed remains ambiguous. Roughly speaking, the Old Testament stresses the former while the New Testament stresses the latter. Jehovah smites, Jesus forgives. It's not *quite* that simple, of course, because there are plenty of hardshell Baptists around who love smiting just as much as any Old Testament prophet, and plenty of Jews who forgive as readily as a Unitarian. But "justice and mercy" remain the poles of the dilemma.

Nobody really resolves this dilemma while he's hale and kicking. When the room starts to darken, it gets easier. The German poet Heinrich Heine, for example, lingered for eight years with a wasting disease thought to be syphilis. He'd been pretty nasty to a number of people in his life—the German government banished him, and he had to defend himself twice in duels—so when his time finally came, it might be supposed he'd be penitent. Not exactly. Just before he died, someone asked him if he had gotten right with the Lord. Heine, who seemed little concerned about the forgiveness of his enemies, expressed a similarly cavalier attitude toward the Most High. "**God will pardon me,**" he shrugged. "**It's his job.**"

Henry David Thoreau, who died six years after Heine, had a similarly flip response to the ultimate question. When his aunt asked him, on his deathbed, if he'd made *his* peace with God, he replied, "**I did not know we had ever quarreled.**" Thoreau was a Transcendentalist, of course, and Heine was a Jew who, for professional reasons, had switched to Lutheranism. Maybe it's easier for the nonorthodox to go out smiling.

YOU CAN'T TELL A BLOKE BY HIS COVER

At the beginning of *Moby Dick,* before the *Pequod* puts out to sea, the narrator, Ishmael, makes the acquaintance of the harpooner Queequeq, who will become his bosom friend on the fateful voyage and whose coffin will become the means of his survival. Imbued with the standard prejudices of his time, Ishmael's first reaction, when discovering that he is to share a bed with a "cannibal," is to shriek for the landlord, and then for angels, to deliver him. When the landlord tells him that the savage is harmless, he repents his hastiness and resolves to make the best of it. Musing that, in spite of his tattoos, the man was "on the whole a clean, comely looking cannibal," Ishmael becomes the soul of rational charity. Queequeg is a human being, after all, with "just as much reason to fear me as I have to be afraid of him." His final admonition to himself, while seeming to flout Christianity, actually serves to vindicate its basic message. Conduct, not creed, is what matters. Thus: **"Better sleep with a sober cannibal than a drunken Christian."** That resolved, the two retire, and as Ishmael later recalls, "I . . . never slept better in my life."

A BETTER WORLD—BUT WHERE?

During the civil rights turmoil of the 1960s, black radicals, becoming impatient with Martin Luther King's nonviolence, turned in frustration to armed resistance. In identifying the spiritual impulse for patience as counterproductive to social change, they were sharing the conceits of thousands of radicals who had come before them and were echoing in particular Karl Marx's opinion of religion.

Marx made his most often quoted comment on religion in 1844 in "Contribution to the Critique of Hegel's Philosophy of Right." There he calls it **"the sign of the oppressed creature," "the soul of soulless conditions,"** and—most famously—**"the opium of the people."** He was getting at what he saw as the tendency of religious people to accept injustice in the here and now in exchange for the promise that, after death, their endurance of misery would be rewarded. Napoleon I, Emperor of the French, had made the same point years before, when he said **"Religion is what keeps the poor from murdering the rich."**

That religion has helped people endure misfortune, including the misfortune of oppressive social systems, may be easily demonstrated. But the idea that religion is inevitably reactionary is a proposal that only the doctrinaire will accept. King's life itself offered evidence to the contrary. So have the experiences of numerous "purifying" and utopian sects, from the Hussites to the Mormons, bent on radically transforming the here and now. H. G. Wells, in his 1946 book *The Happy Turning,* observes that **"Religions are such stuff as dreams are made of."** That's a more inclusive assessment. Some religious dreams, it's quite true, have served as opiates. Others have fomented such radically re-constructive enterprises as social revolution, political reform, and the death of kings.

CHICKEN OR EGG?

The English writer Samuel Butler (1835–1902) is best known for his novel *The Way of All Flesh* and his century's most accomplished utopian satire, *Erewhon.* His interests were wide, however. Among his other writings were a study of Shakespeare's sonnets, a defense of the proposition that Homer was a woman, and a series of extended essays on evolution. Charles Darwin's writings hit Butler's generation like an intellectual tidal wave, and he wrote extensively in an attempt to explain to Darwin's champions the shortcomings of evolutionary theory.

In his first book on evolution, *Life and Habit,* he addressed the question of which came first, chicken or egg, and gave an answer that must have set many a clerical head spinning. The standard churchgoer's answer to the conundrum, of course, was that because God created the animals (see Genesis), hatcher must have preceded hatchee. Butler count-ered this argument with a coy definition: **"A hen is only an egg's way of making another egg."**

Butler had started out training for the clergy but left disillusioned, so his jibe may be construed as evidence of apostasy. So too may a brief definition from his posthumously published notebooks: **"An honest God's the noblest work of man."**

GOD AND MAMMON RECONCILED

At the height of his influence, the American industrialist John D. Rockefeller (1839–1937), the head of gigantic Standard Oil, supervised the refining of approximately 70 percent of all U.S. oil. His personal fortune, the world's largest, was said to exceed one billion dollars—in the era of nickel beers and dollar suits. He had worked hard to accumulate this pile, beginning as a young bookkeeper in the 1860s, but in his eyes labor alone had not done it. The full explanation: **"God gave me my money."**

That sounds a bit smarmy, even hypocritical, but it wasn't. Good Protestant that he was, John D. was simply reflecting the Calvinist doctrine that God favored with "signs of election" those chosen few who were predestined to enter heaven. In Calvin's revolutionary sociology, material wealth served as one of those signs. The idea made hash of Catholicism's traditional respect for poverty, and it helped to justify the capitalist system, which was growing in Europe at the same time as the Protestant Reformation. The linkage is the theme of Max Weber's classic study *The Protestant Ethic and the Spirit of Capitalism*.

As effective as Rockefeller was in justifying the ways of Mammon to God, he also felt obliged to disburse his wealth, believing like Andrew Carnegie that it was as wrong to die rich as to live poor. Hence he became an extraordinarily generous Croesus. His philanthropic contributions still support, among other institutions, the Rockefeller Foundation and the University of Chicago.

PLUMBING THE MIND OF GOD

As the epigraph to his warm and readable life of Albert Einstein, Ronald Clark offers an observation that Einstein made in 1949 in a physics journal: **"I have little patience with scientists who take a board of wood, look for its thinnest part, and drill a great**

number of holes where drilling is easy." Einstein's life work, Clark points out, was just the opposite. Long before he came upon the theory of relativity, which made him famous, he had remarked to the German philosopher Martin Buber that his goal was "**to draw His lines after Him**"—that is, to retrace the geometrical design of the entire universe. Later he told a colleague in Berlin, "**I want to know His thoughts. The rest are details.**" Not exactly the thinnest part of the wood.

In forming this intention—one which he worked to realize his entire life—Einstein was troubled by one conceivable, but unallowable, possibility: that the universe itself was chaotic because God either had no plan or changed the rules as He went along. To Einstein, like the philosopher Spinoza, whom he admired, an orderly universe and the concept of God were inseparable. We might not be able to perceive the order, but that it existed was a matter of scientific no less than religious faith. He believed, as he put it in his most famous formulation, that "**God does not play dice with the world.**"

THE MORE THINGS CHANGE...

One of the oldest tangles in the history of religion is whether, given an omnipotent and all-seeing God, human beings can actually *do* anything at all, that is, whether we have the power to affect circumstances, even our own. If the entire future already exists in the mind of God, isn't His will being done, whether we like it or not and whether or not we're being good, bad, or indifferent? If whatever happens is already known, or "preordained," then isn't the plea "Thy will be done" a mere tautology?

I won't solve this here (as if I could). Instead, I'll give you one of the best question-beggings of the issue I've ever encountered. If you've ever been to an Alcoholics Anonymous meeting, you've already heard it, since it's an unofficial motto of the organization: "**God, give us the serenity to accept the things that cannot be changed, the courage to change the things that can be changed, and the wisdom to know the difference.**" The discerning reader will notice that, as lusciously comforting as this prayer is, it leaves the "wisdom" part up in the air—if we knew the difference between what could and couldn't be changed, we'd already be in the company of the angels.

The quotation, incidentally, didn't originate with AA. They borrowed it from a sermon preached back in the 1940s by the American dean of Protestant thinkers in this century, theologian Reinhold Niebuhr (1892–1971).

AND THE GREATEST OF THESE IS CHARITY

Niebuhr also wrote *The Irony of American History,* a richly thoughtful commentary on the Christian virtues. The Roman Catholic church identifies seven of these, no doubt to buck the influence of the better known, and more easily embraced, seven deadly sins. (The sins are Pride, Wrath, Envy, Lust, Gluttony, Avarice, and Sloth. Pride of place goes, of course, to Pride, which was Satan's sin and nourishes all the others.) The virtues are Faith, Hope, Charity, Justice, Fortitude, Prudence, and Temperance. The first three, collectively known as the theological virtues, Niebuhr glosses as follows:

> **Nothing that is worth doing can be achieved in a lifetime; therefore we must be saved by hope.**
>
> **Nothing which is true or beautiful or good makes complete sense in any immediate context of history; therefore we must be saved by faith.**
>
> **Nothing we do, however virtuous, can be accomplished alone; therefore we are saved by love.**

A CIRCLE OF JERKS

Once shocking and now an old reliable of amateur drama societies, Jean-Paul Sartre's one-act play *No Exit* examines the hopelessness of human existence by pitting against one another three recently deceased strangers. Estelle is a nymphomaniac who drove her lover to suicide by murdering their illegitimate baby. Inez is a lesbian who seduced her cousin's wife, driving *her* to suicide. Garcin is a failed pacifist who betrayed his cause and was shot while trying to flee a military prison. The three meet in hell, which looks suspiciously like a French drawing room, and torture one another by exhibiting doomed desire. Estelle wants Garcin, Inez wants Estelle, Garcin wants to be thought the hero he never was. The mess they make for one another is capsulized in the play's signature line, **"Hell is other people."**

The irony of the action, as well as the existential point, is that the trio imprison themselves in their own definitions. When the door to the drawing room opens toward the end of the play, they are unable to escape their torment by walking through it. As the curtain closes on their frantic, self-deprecating laughter, they embody horribly the inability to accept responsibility, which Sartre identified as the human condition of "bad faith."

ONCE A CATHOLIC, ALWAYS A CATHOLIC

The Spanish-born film director Luis Buñuel (1900–1983) burst upon the European art scene as Salvador Dali's collaborator on the surrealist shocker *Un Chien Andalou* (1928). Two years later, *L'Age d'Or* established his reputation as an iconoclast and showed audiences for the first time his obsessive distrust of ecclesiastical and social convention. That distrust informed many of his later masterpieces, such as *Viridiana* (1961) and *The Discreet Charm of the Bourgeoisie* (1972), and it turned with special vengeance, throughout Buñuel's career, on the Roman Catholic church, in which he was raised.

Sometimes his attack on the church was blunt and direct but more often than not it displayed the nervous irony you would expect from someone educated by Jesuits and defrocked, as it were, by Salvador Dali. He himself was perfectly aware of this irony. **"Thank God,"** he was often quoted, **"I am still an atheist."**

JUST THE FACTS, MA'AM

When Nietzsche declared in his masterwork *Thus Spoke Zarathustra* (1885) that **"God is dead,"** he was doing no more than making public what thousands of his generation already knew: the verities of the

Christian religion were on the run, chased from the European consciousness by Marx and Darwin. John Lennon performed a similar, and similarly resented, informational service eight decades later when, at the height of Beatlemania, he announced, **"The Beatles are now more popular than Jesus Christ."**

In both cases the bearer of bad tidings was assumed to be pleased with the news. That's unfair to both Nietzsche and Lennon. That God and Jesus were "dead" in a box office sense was an indisputable fact of modern society, but stating a fact is hardly the same as relishing it. If Nietzsche's and Lennon's comments sounded cynical, it's good to remember that most cynics are idealists with broken hearts.

The subtlety was lost on outraged Christians in the 1960s, as it was lost to haters of Nietzsche at the turn of the century. His death in 1900, possibly from syphilis, followed a decade of increasing derangement and erratic writing. The brilliant unevenness of his later work was often dismissed as ranting, and his famous declaration was snidely reviewed in a bathroom graffito:

> **"God is dead." (Nietzsche, 1885)**
> **"Nietzsche is dead." (God, 1900)**

Birds, Bees, and Other Distractions

Men and Women

THAT (ALMOST) NO ONE CAN DENY

Aside from occasional nods to the old saw: "**You can't live with 'em and you can't live without 'em,**" the world's thinkers have tended to agree that the division of the human race into two genders serves a useful, if not always clearly defined, purpose. Such was the opinion of Nathaniel Hawthorne in *The Blithedale Romance*. That chatty, seamy little study of free love is hardly a strong argument for marriage, but it does suggest it may be the lesser of available evils. Why? Because "**man is a wretch without woman**" and "**woman is a monster without man.**" Hawthorne's contemporary Henry Wheeler Shaw, who wrote under the nom de ribnudge Josh Billings, seemed to agree. "**Man without woman,**" he pronounced, "**would be like playing checkers alone.**" This century's Herman Hupfeld repeated the thought in his most famous song, "As Time Goes By," where—if you will recall your last viewing of *Casablanca*—"**Man must have his mate, that no one can deny.**"

Denials of this idea are rare outside of monasteries, although a particularly good one emerged in the 1970s, as part of the feminist reassessment of the human order. Women and men needing each other? Not according to this bumper sticker: "**A woman without a man is like a fish without a bicycle.**" It's Salvador Dali, edited by Gertrude Stein.

THE FASCINATION OF WHAT'S NOT DIFFICULT

The *Canadian Encyclopedia* calls Charlotte Whitton "one of this century's most colorful and controversial women." She was also one of its most paradoxical politicians: a social conservative who promoted child welfare laws, a feminist who opposed liberal divorce laws, and a five term mayor of Ottawa who argued against married women seeking employment. Born in 1896, she ran her country's Council on Child Welfare for over twenty years, fighting tirelessly for more professional treatment of neglected children. Her resistance to government spending for the unemployed, however, mystified her fellow minions of the welfare state and led to her resignation from the council in 1941. In the 1950s and 1960s, as Canada's first woman mayor, she continued to shock people with her contradictory politics, so outraging the opposition at one point that she and a male colleague came to blows.

Of Whitton's many memorable public comments, the most enduring is her assessment of women's abilities. "**Whatever women do they must do twice as well as men to be thought half as good. Luckily, this is not difficult.**" Her biographers, P. T. Rooke and R. L. Schnell, give a good idea of her popular legacy in the title of their volume: *No Bleeding Heart*. No shrinking violet either.

DUSKY BEAUTIES BOUND

In one of his early "Barrack-Room Ballads," Rudyard Kipling penned a classic of phallocentrism: "**A woman is only a woman, but a good cigar is a smoke.**" Whether or not he recognized the autoerotic connotations of the expressed preference—or the attendant misogyny—those elements certainly exist in the text, and it's not shocking that the line should bring smiles to militant bachelors who confuse commitment with castration.

The comparison of pleasures that is hinted at in this line is spelled out extensively in the poem. Entitled "The Betrothed," it's a fifty-line internal debate by a man who is about to marry his "loving lass" Maggie but has been given an ultimatum before the wedding: either the stogies go, or I do. Swinging back and forth between Love and "the great god Nick-o'-Teen," he makes much of the physical beauty question, gradually realizing that, although Maggie will get "grey and dour and old," the cigars will be in effect forever young, because you can throw a dead one away for "another as perfect and ripe and brown." Besides, Maggie obviously has a mind of her own, while the cigars are as nicely submissive as servant girls:

> **Open the old cigar-box—let me consider awhile;**
> **Here is a mild Manila—there is a wifely smile.**
> **Which is the better portion—bondage bought with a ring,**
> **Or a harem of dusky beauties, fifty tied in a string?**

Hardly seems much of a contest, when you put it that way, and the "betrothed" ends up throwing Maggie over to honor his "first sworn vows."

With its commodity fetishism, oral fixation, and hints of bondage, the poem is a perfect embodiment of puerile chauvinism—exactly what you would expect from an army barracks. But the narrator's decision was not Kipling's. Two years after "The Betrothed" appeared, he got married.

AS CHEAPLY AS ONE, HELL

A self-described philosophical libertarian, Henry Louis Mencken had little good to say about marriage during most of his journalistic career, seeing it—as so many young men with more spunk than patience see it—as a rose-strewn dead end for free spirits. Alert particularly to the economic compromises that accompany joint budget making,

Mencken ridiculed the "happy" husband as a master of self-delusion: **"No man is genuinely happy, married, who has to drink worse whiskey than he used to drink when he was single."** That comes from his fourth book of *Prejudices,* published in 1924. Six years later, at the age of fifty, Mencken married for the first time—a woman from Alabama who, sadly, died only five years after the wedding.

DIE BLAUE BLUME REBORN

Among the most durable of the Romantics' delusions is the intoxicating notion of the soul mate—the idea that of the millions of human beings available to a given individual for discourse, emotional interspicuity, or copulation, only *one* exists whose bond to the subject is cosmically planned. It's a delusion newly discovered by every generation, and although most of us abandon it, along with our prom dresses and Christmas stockings, around voting age, a precious few sustain the dream all their lives.

Innocent as the soul mate idea is, though, it does once in a while generate a great sentence. **"I want someone, walking with me through a sea of grass, who would point out a little mimosa flower in the distance which I was going to point out to him."** Cosmic, yes? The writer is one Darsan Wang, about whom I know only that he lived in Michigan in 1972; wrote a novel, *Stationary Front,* about that time; submitted it to the publisher for whom I then worked; and was told, against my better judgment, that it didn't fit our "current publishing needs." I reproduce the book's most arresting line partly to atone for my boss's rigidity and partly because, to paraphrase *Citizen Kane*'s Mr. Bernstein, hardly a month has gone by since 1972 that I haven't thought about that little mimosa flower.

SIDE BY SIDE

Before thirty or so, which is to say before the age of reason, lovers often suppose they can obliterate the outside world by gazing intently, with utter honesty, into each other's eyes. Soul mates against a hostile universe, mystical union, that sort of thing. Once you've done this a few times and wake up to discover the rent is still due, you change your tune. As you age, if you're lucky you learn to love, as the old parlor-piano song has it, "side by side." Just as reassuring when you get the hang of it, and you spend less time bumping into furniture.

Dancer Ginger Rogers said it well. **"When two people love each other, they don't look at each other. They look in the same direction."** A more melancholy version of the same nugget comes from Rainer Maria Rilke, the German poet who tended to see pretty much everything in a yellow light. In his collection of philosophical musings *Letters to a Young Poet,* he writes, **"Love consists in this, that two solitudes protect and border and salute each other."**

AH, INNOCENCE!

In Hollywood's old days, when you could be suggestive without being salacious and still get box office, the love affair between Gary Cooper and Ingrid Bergman in the 1943 movie *For Whom the Bell Tolls* portrayed the innocence of awakening sexuality with remarkable charm. Cooper plays Robert Jordan, American idealist turned munitions expert for the Republicans in the Spanish Civil War. Bergman is (stretch your imagination now) the Spanish peasant girl Maria, who falls under the spell of the lanky *americano.* In Hemingway's book, their courting and subsequent lovemaking take about three trees' worth of paper to accomplish and include the famous twaddle about the Earth moving as they intertwine. In the movie, their most memorable exchange comes just before their first kiss. I'm new to this, admits Maria. **"Where do the noses go?"** You get racier lines these days in Saturday cartoons.

They figure out where the noses go, but neither that nor a moving Earth makes for happiness. Sacrificing Bergman for his ideals, just like Rick Blaine in *Casablanca,* Jordan covers his retreating comrades from a Fascist advance, losing his life in the process. We never find out what happens to Maria, although Bergman herself makes out fine. She wins her first Academy Award, for *Gaslight,* the following year, then goes to Europe with her lover, Roberto Rossellini. Their daughter Isabella has carried on her mother's tradition of shocking the rubes in David Lynch's ugly little number *Blue Velvet*—where the noses, thank you very much, go anywhere they please.

CLEOPATRA'S NOSE

The Ptolemaic dynasty of Egypt began when one of Alexander the Great's generals, Ptolemy Soter, declared himself king in 305 B.C. It ended not quite three centuries later, when his descendant Ptolemy XV was murdered by followers of the Roman general Octavian. This last Ptolemy was the son of Julius Caesar and the Egyptian queen Cleopatra—the last and most famous of seven Cleopatras—who had also been the mistress of Caesar's friend Mark Antony and thus opposed to Antony's rival, the invading Octavian.

In her zeal to consolidate her own power, Cleopatra used both sex and murder with deft abandon. When Caesar reached Egypt in 48 B.C., she was already involved in a struggle for the throne with her brother, Ptolemy XIII. She got rid of him, married their younger brother (Ptolemy XIV), but also took up with Caesar on the side, even following him to Rome, where she stayed until he was killed in 44. Then it was back to Egypt, a judicious alliance with Mark Antony, and their Hollywood-style love affair, which lasted until their defeat by Octavian in 31. After that disaster, she offered herself to Octavian and, when that failed, to an asp. The asp accepted, she died, and Egypt fell under the dominion of Rome, with Octavian as the first Roman emperor.

The queen's intimacies with Caesar and Antony have fascinated dramatists for centuries. They also profoundly influenced the course of history, for without her intrigues, there might have been no Roman Empire. The French philosopher Blaise Pascal had it right when he wrote in his *Pensées,* **"The nose of Cleopatra. Had it been shorter, the face of the earth would have been changed."**

PUCKERING UP, NEW STYLE

Lauren Bacall, née Betty Joan Perske, was nineteen years old when she was cast opposite Humphrey Bogart in *To Have and Have Not.* The role included the opportunity to make one of the most memorable first impressions in American movie history, and she milked it for all it was worth. Lounging lustily against a door jamb, she sidles into the room, and into Bogart's wide-eyed ken, with the curt query **"Anybody got a match?"** Rather than lighting her cigarette himself, he throws her a pack, she snags it out of the air, and a sexual tension is put in motion that will slither within their dialogue throughout the film.

That entry scene is only marginally less famous than a balancing doorway scene later in the movie. Bacall's "Slim" has just kissed Bogart's Morgan, because she has been "wondering whether I'd like it." She does, they try it again, she smiles that "it's even better when you help," and then, walking out, she delivers the famous "whistle" speech:

> **You know you don't have to act with me, Steve. You don't have to say anything and you don't have to do anything. Oh, maybe, just whistle. You know how to whistle, don't you, Steve? You just put your lips together and blow.**

The husky suggestiveness with which she delivers this advice, not to mention the double-entendre in the word *blow,* make this scene at once restrained and delightfully racy. Contrast this with the mattress sweating that passes for "sexiness" today, and you will see the cost we have paid in sophistication for "explicit" treatments.

BEHIND CLOSED DOORS

Mrs. Patrick Campbell (1865–1940), England's leading actress at the turn of the century, established her reputation in 1893 as Paula in Arthur Wing Pinero's popular drama *The Second Mrs. Tanqueray.* A high-brow's darling, she galvanized audiences with portrayals of Hedda Gabler, Ophelia, and Lady Macbeth, yet was also able to demonstrate a comic flair as Eliza in Bernard Shaw's 1914 *Pygmalion.* Like her longtime cor-respondent (if not co-respondent) Shaw, her views on life, including romantic life, were ahead of her time. Here, for example, are her thoughts on sexual "eccentricity": **"It doesn't matter what you do in the bedroom, as long as you don't do it in the street and frighten the horses."** That may not sound very daring today, but you must remember that it was said decades before John Lennon, the "liberated Beatle," saw fit to ask, of a far less prudish generation, **"Why don't we do it in the road?"**

OR IS THAT ''NO-KISS OFF''?

Bette Davis began her film career in 1931, as a twenty-three-year-old ingenue from the Provincetown Players. She first signed with Universal, but studio head Carl Laemmle thought she had, as he put it, **"as much sex appeal as Slim Summerville,"** and by the following year she had moved to Warner Brothers. There in 1932, in a forgettable melodrama called *The Cabin in the Cotton,* she got the chance to deliver a four-star kiss-off line. Playing the first in a series of sultry Southern belles, she deflates an admirer by drawling, **"I'd love to kiss you, but I just washed my hair."** Davis must have delivered thousands of lines in over fifty years on the screen. Given her reputation as an off-camera hard case, it's not surprising she thought of this one as her favorite.

MOON-SPOON-JUNE

People get married in June because the ancient Romans established the tradition: June was the month sacred to Juno, queen of the gods and patroness of marriage. They don't get married (or didn't, up until this apostate century) in May because it was thought unlucky to jump the gun and cheat Juno of her due. She already had enough cheating to worry about, with the superlecher Jupiter as her husband.

Back around the turn of the century, when these things seemed to matter more than they do today, the American journalist William James Lampton (1859–1917) enshrined the June wedding in a lighthearted poem entitled, appropriately enough, "June Weddings." The full text is kicking around the Great Newspaper Verse Morgue in the Sky, but one couplet survives to grace quotation books:

> **Same old slippers, same old rice.**
> **Same old glimpse of Paradise.**

An Ohioan by birth, Lampton worked for most of his career on mid-western newspapers but also contributed sparklers like the above to New York rags, and ended up dying in the City. He had spent some time in Kentucky, which he immortalized in another two-liner. He called the Bluegrass State a place

> **Where the corn is full of kernels**
> **And the colonels full of corn.**

SEPARATE BUT EQUAL

Those who make a go of marriage understand that one plus one equals neither two nor one, but ... one plus one. Among these happy souls was the English wit and divine Sydney Smith (1771–1845). Much of Smith's humor reveals a highly developed sense of the absurd. His best recorded description of marriage shows he also had a lot of common sense. A good marriage, he said, was like **"a pair of shears, so joined that they cannot be separated, often moving in opposite directions, yet always punishing anyone who comes between them."** It's a kind of Marxist cell attitude toward nonbelievers. Debate like hell with your fellow Marxists but adopt a united front for outsiders. It hasn't always worked well for Marxists, but evidently it worked well for Smith. He and his wife, Catherine, stayed together for over forty years.

SHE STOOPED TO CONQUER

The first woman ever to serve in Britain's Parliament, Lady Astor, née Nancy Witcher (1879–1964), entered that august men's club resolved to needle, rather than revere, its traditions. Her witty interruptions were so frequent that once, when she claimed to have listened to a debate for hours before breaking in, a colleague replied, "**Yes, we *heard* you listening.**" Her feistiness on the floor was entirely in character, for she never felt obliged to prove herself an equal to men. Her celebrated estimation of marriage, for example, was "**I married beneath me. All women do.**"

What her husband, Viscount Waldorf Astor, thought of this line is hard to say, although it seems not to have noticeably marred the union. They were married in 1906 and stayed together until his death in 1952. The *Dictionary of National Biography* says the last few years were troubled because Lady Astor in 1945 vacated the post she had occupied since 1919. While she was plenty used to being around the house, as it were, she got irritable when that house was not the Commons.

BUMBLING INTO HOT WATER

In Dickens's *Oliver Twist,* the workhouse official Mr. Bumble marries a widow, Mrs. Corney, for her property and soon discovers he's written himself a heavy sentence. As sharp tongued as she is domineering, she makes his fall into comfort a bed of nails. She's also a thief, and under the curious judicial system of the presuffragette era, that makes hubby Bumble her unwitting accomplice. When it's discovered that she has filched a pawn ticket and sold the goods that it represented for private gain, the investigating authorities condemn her husband as well as her. Pleading innocence, Bumble is informed that he is actually "the more guilty" in the eye of the law. Why? Because "the law supposes that your wife acts under your direction." Appalled, Bumble splutters in frustration, "**If the law supposes that, the law is a ass—a idiot.**" He's not exactly a protofeminist, but it's a line that might have tickled Gloria Steinem.

THE OLD IN-OUT, IN-OUT

Woolworth heiress Barbara Hutton got married and divorced so many times that even the standard sources lost count. Christopher Cerf and Victor Navasky's "compendium of authoritative misinformation," *The Experts Speak,* assigns her seven weddings and seven misses. *Who's*

Who stops at her sixth, to Baron Gottfried von Kramm (1955), failing to mention a brief hook-up in the 1960s to a Vietnamese prince, Doan Vinh de Champacak. Everybody agrees her third husband was actor Cary Grant, whom she divorced in 1945 with the promise "**I will never marry again.**" When she blew that prediction by marrying Porfirio Rubirosa (1963), writer Phyllis Battelle grinned maliciously, "**For her fifth wedding, the bride wore black and carried a Scotch and soda.**"

Also known for his multiple alliances was swing-era band leader Artie Shaw. When asked why, he shrugged winsomely, "**You have no idea of the people I *didn't* marry.**"

PUTTING ASUNDER

The Protestant Reformation of the sixteenth century made divorce easier for Europeans to obtain than had been the case under Rome, but it took decades for alimony to enter the picture. Latin *alimonia* means literally "nourishment." Not until the middle of the seventeenth century did it come to mean the financial nourishment that a husband sent his divorced wife. It wasn't long after that, however, that the cynicism attaching to the word made itself felt. By the 1720s, the English actress and playwright Susannah Centlivre was already quipping, "**A wound in the reputation of an English woman, they say, only lets in Alimony.**"

Modern cynics have only added to that estimation. Among the most acerbic comments on the tradition of nourishing an ex, one may note H. L. Mencken's description of it as "**the ransom that the happy pay to the devil,**" and a personal reflection by contemporary humorist Lewis Grizzard. After a number of unhappy (and costly) trips to the altar, he observed, "**I don't think I'll get married again. I'll just find a woman I don't like and give her a house.**"

COMMON LAW, COMMON SENSE

The first major "palimony" suit in history took place in the spring of 1979, when Michelle Triola, the longtime live-in lover of actor Lee

Marvin, sued him for financial support after their breakup. Although they had never been legally married, she argued, reasonably enough, that since the arrangement had provided him the same conjugal advantages (bed, board, and homemaking) that a legal marriage usually provides a husband, she was entitled to the same privileges as a divorced wife. After a California jury agreed, she celebrated by announcing, "**If a man wants to leave a toothbrush at my house, he can damn well marry me.**" A word to the wiseguy.

AND ON THE DOWN SIDE...

The hearts-and-flowers type of Valentine card, popular from the seventeenth through the nineteenth centuries, has been supplemented in our jaundiced time by ironic "novelty" cards, stressing sexual or dyspeptic sentiments at the expense of the romantic. One of my favorite (repeatable) messages from this relatively recent assortment accompanies a picture of a young lover walking into a garden. To judge from the front of the card, you'll find some lame "Roses are red" update on the inside. What you do find is this: "**Nobody loves me. I'm going into the garden and eat worms.**"

chapter 3

Making
Ends Meet

Money and Economy

BUCK WORSHIP

Washington Irving (1783–1859), America's first successful professional writer, made numerous contributions to the national folklore, the best-known being the characters of Diedrich Knickerbocker, Rip Van Winkle, and Ichabod Crane. He was also responsible for the expression **"almighty dollar,"** the insolvent radical's instant proof that Americans are more greedy than other folks. It appears in Irving's travel sketch "The Creole Village." On a trip to Louisiana, the New York author was delighted to find rural hamlets that had not yet caught the national fever for gain, and he expressed his astonishment sardonically in this passage:

> **The almighty dollar, that great object of universal devotion throughout our land, seems to have no genuine devotees in these peculiar villages; and unless some of its missionaries penetrate there, and erect banking houses and other pious shrines, there is no knowing how long**

the inhabitants may remain in their present state of contented poverty.

LAST OF THE RED HOT MAMAS

The career of stage phenomenon Sophie Tucker (1884–1966) is an object lesson in turning necessity into virtue. Born in Russia to Jewish parents, she entered the United States as part of the turn-of-the-century "new immigration," worked briefly in her parents' Connecticut restaurant, then was bitten by the showbiz bug as a teenager while playing piano accompaniment for her sister at amateur shows. Since she weighed nearly 150 pounds at age thirteen, catcalls for the "fat girl" were common, and she quickly turned this annoyance into an advantage, playing for laughs as a way to get exposure.

In 1906 she moved to New York, where the "big mama" routine made her a star. On vaudeville, in English music halls, and in the country's most fashionable nightclubs, Sophie Tucker delighted audiences for the next six decades with a unique blend of brassy songs and saucy humor. Hollywood captured her talents in musical films. British royalty requested command performances. Whether she was cooing a sad ballad or belting out a racy jazz tune, she was, in the words of a 1928 signature tune, "The Last of the Red Hot Mamas."

In the early 1950s, as she was approaching seventy, Tucker gave a lightly cynical review of what she had learned. "**From birth to eighteen a girl needs good parents. From eighteen to thirty-five she needs good looks, from thirty-five to fifty-five a good personality, and from fifty-five on she needs cash.**" She'd made a similar comment, with more economy, years before: "**I've been poor and I've been rich. Believe me, rich is better.**"

OUT LIKE FLYNN

Errol Flynn, the Australian-born charmer whose autobiography is entitled *My Wicked, Wicked Ways,* was as widely known for his womanizing and vodka intake as he was for the roles of derring-do that made him a star. His friends also knew him as what a Republican would call "fiscally irresponsible." Endowed with the eternal adolescent's lust for life, and little better at managing money than he had been when he left his native Tasmania, he once admitted, **"My difficulty is in reconciling my gross habits with my net income."**

His closest friends knew this best, and few were closer than his fellow actor and drinking buddy David Niven. For a time, the two shared a beach house, which they affectionately called Cirrhosis-by-the-Sea. The British actor said that his housemate had a bizarre kind of reliability: **"The great thing about Errol was that you knew precisely where you were with him—because he *always* let you down."** That was a fitting comment on a broadcast that Flynn made to his former countrymen. There were rumors he had escaped from Down Under after killing a man, and it was a certainty that he had fled with bills unpaid. In the broadcast, he owned up: **"If there's anyone listening to whom I owe money, I'm prepared to forget it if you are."** He was, as you might say, a brass act.

TRANSFER PAYMENTS, ANYONE?

A hundred years before Voltaire fought conventional thinking in France, Francis Bacon (1561–1626) did the same thing across the English Channel. In his major philosophical work, the *Novum Organum* of 1620, he rejected the syllogistic reasoning of his contemporaries and proposed experience as the true font of human knowledge. Voltaire was only one of many Enlightenment thinkers who credited him with virtually inventing the scientific method.

He was an essayist too, and in a typically pithy essay on "Seditions and Troubles," he expressed a political opinion that was every bit as odd in his day as the idea that nature could best be understood by observation. In an age of massive fortunes and crushing poverty, he dared to write, **"Money is like muck, not good except it be spread."** Since *muck* had meant both *manure* and *money* since the fourteenth century, Bacon wasn't being original here, but his comment still casts a solid, protocommunist light on "filthy lucre."

THE BERNSTEIN PROVISO

The fact that *Citizen Kane* was put together by a smartass twenty-five-year-old who had never made a movie before only adds to the *Kane*—and the Welles—mystique. If its director had been a fifty-year veteran, it would still be the most interesting American movie ever made. Whether you concentrate on the story or the cinematography, the script or the acting, it's impossible to name another Hollywood production in which everything fits together with such precision.

The *Kane* script, done by Welles and Herman Mankiewicz, contains countless gems that do not work out of context. "I think it would be fun to run a newspaper," for example, means nothing unless you've seen George Coulouris say it. The same with Dorothy Comingore's "You gotta love me," and the entire cast's mysteriously repeated "Rosebud." Of the lines that do transcend the text, my favorite comes from Kane's right-hand man, Mr. Bernstein, played superbly by film newcomer Everett Sloane. The reporter who is attempting to discover who the recently deceased Kane "really" was tells Bernstein, "He sure made a lot of money." **"It's not hard to make a lot of money,"** Bernstein replies, **"if all you want to do is to make a lot of money."** It was Kane's tragedy, the old friend implies, that he wanted more.

So did Welles, by the way. *Citizen Kane,* amazingly enough, was a consolation prize. The story he had first broached to RKO was an adaptation of Joseph Conrad's *Heart of Darkness.* They told him it would be too expensive. Welles never did make that film, or anything else with nearly the brilliance of his opening diamond.

THE EMBARRASSMENT OF RICHES

The trouble with wealth, speaking from a strictly practical point of view, is not that it is so envied and so unseemly but that it weighs so heavily upon the resources of its owner. Those who have never tasted luxury imagine that a new Porsche, a Picasso in the drawing room, a pied-à-terre in the Trump Tower, will bring them ease rather than aggravation. If that were true, the Porsches, Picassos, and Trumps of the world would all be contented souls. One glance at history tells you they are not.

The problem is not simply that owning goods feeds upon itself, generating desires in a competitive frenzy to outdo other owners. It's that goods themselves are an endless responsibility. They must be not only paid for but also stored, insured, and publicly admired—all of which costs not just money but personal freedom. If a man with a fortune **"cannot make himself easier and freer than those who are not,"** James Boswell once wrote in his journal, **"he gains nothing."** Nothing except glittering baggage that must be attended to.

In the non-European world, where poverty has never had quite the stigma that it bears in the "get-rich-quick" zone, sages often remark on the tyranny of goods. According to an old Persian proverb, **"The larger a man's roof, the more snow it collects."** Kahlil Gibran's Prophet, in his discussion of "Houses," laments the lust for comfort as a **"stealthy thing that enters the house a guest, and then becomes a host, and then a master."** Compare our own Ralph Waldo Emerson, whose appreciation of Eastern philosophy affected all his thinking. In his poem "Ode to Channing," he scorns the acquisitiveness of his day with the fearsome words **"Things are in the saddle, and ride mankind."**

IT ALL DEPENDS ON HOW YOU LOOK AT IT

The nineteenth-century naturalist John Muir, the planet's first ecoactivist, hiked through thousands of miles of American back country, lobbied feverishly for wilderness preservation, and published classic descriptions of Yosemite Valley and the national parks. His contemporary railroad baron E. H. Harriman helped to subdue Muir's verdant paradise with networks of steel and in the process accumulated one of the greatest personal fortunes of the Gilded Age. He could have bought and sold Muir twenty times before breakfast, but to Muir this was a sign of failure, not success. In true Thoreauvian fashion, Muir once grinned, **"I am richer than E. H. Harriman. I have all the money I want and he hasn't."**

GOD'S OWN DREAMWORLD

New York's Radio City Music Hall typifies Art Deco architecture on the grand scale. The largest, and one of the most lavish, indoor theaters in the world, it opened in 1932, at the depth of the Depression, and throughout that period of dismay and subsequent decades, it represented the glittering excess of an "all-singing, all-dancing" Never Never Land, where even in the harshest times people could dare to dream. You might be poor, but inside that escapist's paradise, with the Rockettes kicking and the Lalique chandeliers gleaming, you felt as close to royalty as a good democracy would allow.

When henchmen of Progress threatened to raze the place in the 1970s, therefore, a sense of outrage swept the city. Thanks to public and private support, the theater was saved. Henry Geldzahler, the cultural affairs commissioner whose outrage was as visible as anyone's, explained appreciatively that the conservationists' success was a tribute to hard cash as much as soft-focus memories: Reflecting on the sheer scale of the famous landmark, he said, **"It's the theater God would have built if he had the money."** *Geldzahler,* maybe not so incidentally, means money counter.

THE SECOND ADAM

The chief insight of Adam Smith's revolutionary volume *The Wealth of Nations* (1776) is that selfishness, in a capitalist economy, tends toward the public good. In Smith's classic description of the laissez-faire faith, the activity of thousands of grasping individuals leads not, as the humanitarian might suppose, to oppression and anarchy, but to a natural rearrangement of resources, such that everyone ends up doing what he does best, goods and services are sold at their optimum (or "fair market") price, and competition creates social equilibrium. The controlling mechanism in this blissful state is Smith's famous "invisible hand," which turns private greed into public gain.

To Smith, this paradox was at the heart of a healthy economy, and attempts to regulate "fairness" by eliminating greed inevitably made matters worse. "**Greed is good,**" as the shady financier Gordon Gecko says in the film *Wall Street*. As Smith said, it was part of human nature—indeed, as he implied in a pithy metaphor, it was part of nature itself. "**Nobody ever saw a dog make a fair and deliberate exchange of one bone for another with another dog.**" In a dog-eat-dog world, Smith concluded, the role of government was to leave the dogs alone to work out their own most efficient allocation of scarce resources. That this sometimes led to one dog getting fat and the other starving was a blip on the chart in the Larger Scheme of Things.

RULES? WHAT RULES?

Before Congress began regulating industries around the turn of the century, American capitalism was pretty much a free-for-all, with the only checks on greedy or unscrupulous behavior being provided by the principal industrialists' sense of fairness. In some of them, this was well developed, but in others it was not even embryonic, and the attitude of this latter, venal group—the so-called robber barons—strongly influenced popular perceptions of business in the Gilded Age.

Probably the line that most blatantly expresses the robber baron mentality was railroader William Vanderbilt's response to a reporter who asked what consideration his company gave to the public welfare: "**The public be damned,**" he replied—meaning that the public knew zip about running a railroad and wouldn't care about Vanderbilt's profit even if it did. An equally telling, though less often quoted, admission is attributed to another railroad king, Collis P. Huntington. Huntington was a founder of the Central Pacific Railroad, which met the Union Pacific at Promontory Point, Utah, in 1869. Tradition says that as an explanation of "fair competition," he offered this image: "**Whatever is not nailed down is mine. Whatever I can pry loose is not nailed down.**"

. . .

THE BANKERS DUNNIT

Economists have been debating for sixty years what *really* caused the Great Depression of the 1930s. Some combination, they all agree, of overproduction, underconsumption, stock speculation, panic selling, and shortened credit—but what combination isn't exactly clear. The conventional wisdom, however, is very clear. (Conventional wisdom always is—that's how it gets to be conventional.) It says that the money barons down on Wall Street caused the Crash with their reckless margin buying and speculative greed, and that the rest of us—who only wanted to be left alone to buy our washing machines on the installment plan— were sucked into the hole in their wake. The bankers and brokers jumped off the cliff first; the country followed.

A collection of quirky quotes is not the place to set this simplistic interpretation right, so I'll settle for giving the best nutshell description of the given wisdom I know. It comes from humorist Will Rogers, whose sympathy for the little man was well known, and whose sideswipes at politicians did as much as the films of Frank Capra or Busby Berkeley to make the Depression era a little less depressing. Here's how he described the causal link between stock plunges and everybody else's thin soup: **"Let Wall Street have a nightmare and the whole country has to help get them back in bed again."**

THE TRUTH HURTS

Back in the bad old, pre-Ralph Nader days, the chairman of General Motors, Thomas Murphy, let slip an admission that branded him instantly as a conscienceless grasper. **"General Motors is not in the business of making cars. General Motors is in the business of making money."** You could hear the gasps from Motor City to the Rio Grande, but personally I never understood the ruckus. If I recall my Samuelson correctly, *all* businesses are in the business of making money: Without the profit motive, you might as well be in Bulgaria. In laying bare what other business leaders were dressing up in frilly ad slogans (like Du Pont's **"Better things for better living through chemistry"**),

Murphy was really guilty of nothing worse than telling the truth. Of course, in a country that believes capitalism is God's own economic system, that is more than enough to get you denounced as a philistine.

KROCING THE COMPETITION

To win at the world's most popular board game, Monopoly, you must compete so effectively against the other players that eventually you alone are left standing. The economic lesson is unambiguous. Modern capitalism thrives on competition, and the fiercer the better. In a system where every winner implies a loser, crushing the other guy isn't a side effect of success; it *is* success.

Andrew Carnegie defended this give-no-quarter approach to business by explaining, "**The first man gets the oyster, the second man gets the shell.**" Cosmetics tycoon Charles Revson echoed the idea with a vengeance when he said, "**I don't meet competition. I crush it.**" So did the founder of McDonald's, the legendary Ray Kroc, who said of his competitors, "**If they were drowning I'd put a hose in their mouth.**" Faced with that kind of honesty, it's easy to agree with broadcast executive David Sarnoff's assessment: "**Competition brings out the best in products and the worst in people.**"

WHAT PAGE IN SAMUELSON WAS THAT?

There's a tee shirt going the rounds down here in Texas that ought to be required reading for freshman economics courses. Maybe it's a teensy bit simplistic, but no more so than the textbooks that define modern capitalism as a type of "free enterprise." The shirt displays the following definitions:

> **Socialism: You have two cows. You keep one and give the other one to the government.**
> **Communism: You give both of them to the government and they give you milk.**
> **Fascism: The government takes both cows and sells you milk.**

Capitalism: You keep one cow, sell the other one, and buy a bull.

Another definition of economic systems that matches these for pithiness is a joke that was popular in Poland just before *glasnost*. "**What's the difference between capitalism and communism? Capitalism is the exploitation of man by man. Communism is the reverse.**"

LE GRAND COLBERT

Every taxee knows how much the government's bite hurts, so it's always nice to hear a taxman admit it. This is Jean Baptiste Colbert (1619–1683), Louis XIV's finance minister, on the only thing that Ben Franklin said was as sure as death. "**The art of taxation consists of plucking the goose so you get the largest amount of feathers with the smallest amount of hissing.**"

Colbert knew whereof he spoke. For the last twenty years of his life, he ran France's entire internal budget, supervising among other things the fostering of industry, the establishment of merchant adventurer companies, and the overhaul of the tariff system so it would support the mercantilist policies with which he was identified. That would have been plenty for most administrators, but "*le grand* Colbert," as he was known, also founded fine arts and science academies, revamped the navy, directed the rewriting of legal codes, and gave Paris the Tuileries Gardens, the Hotel des Invalides, and half the Louvre. Deliver that kind of legacy and you can put up with a few ticked-off geese.

A DEFINITION YOU CAN REMEMBER

To distinguish between a depression and a recession, economists typically haul out their calculators. In a recession, housing starts are more than 8.6 percent down for two and a half consecutive quarters; when unemployment reaches 12.34 percent, you've got a depression, unless at the same time GNP is more than 42 percent of the slope of the Laffer curve and the moon is in Aries—that sort of thing. Harry Truman's definition was much simpler. **"It's a recession when your neighbor loses his job. It's a depression when you lose yours."**

HOW MANY ZEROES IS THAT?

John Paul Getty (1892–1976), the son of an oil man, used a grubstake given him by his father to enter the family trade in Oklahoma. By the time he was twenty-three he had made his first million, and by the time he died, he was worth in the neighborhood of one billion. I say neighborhood because the figure is an estimate, and Getty himself knew it was fuzzy. **"If you can count your money,"** he once confessed, **"you don't have a billion dollars."**

Countable or not, the money was there. He used it principally to collect art and fund a museum—the aptly named J. Paul Getty Museum in Malibu, California. With an endowment of $750 million, it is the richest museum in the world.

WELCOME TO THE GILDED YEARS

Since few Americans can now rely on their children to take care of them in their old age, providing retirement security has become a national industry, while worrying about how long your life savings will last has become pretty much a universal ailment. Night club comic Henry Youngman a few years ago put a bittersweet twist on this growing problem. He wasn't worried about his sunset years. **"I've got all the money I'll ever need,"** he mused appreciatively, **"just so long as I die by four o'clock."**

MORE BANG FOR THE BUCK

Everybody knows you need money to make war. The simpler-minded critics of militarism also believe this truism's flip side—that you (or rather, the wealthy) need war to make money. Indeed, among the most ideological, the entire purpose of war is to make the wealthy wealthier—and, incidentally, to slaughter the working class in the process. Jean-Paul Sartre stated it obviously in 1951: **"When the rich make war, it's the poor who die."** Before that, the British peace movement, brimming with working class solidarity until the bombs started to drop, made the same point in a vivid slogan: **"A bayonet is a weapon with a worker at each end."**

A more sophisticated assessment of the connection between war and money was put forward by British politician David Lloyd George when, in 1914, he predicted the outcome of the Great War. In his view, the strength of financial resources—not just human resources—would determine the winner. More succinctly, **"The last one hundred million pounds will win."**

IF YOU CAN'T BUY LOVE, WHAT ABOUT HATE?

Most rich people agree, at least on paper, that the advantages of wealth are not the dollars themselves but what those dollars (or deutsche marks, or yen) will *do* for you once you have them. That is, money is good because you can trade it in on more goods, more leisure, a better world—either for yourself or for others. Duh. A rare exception to this obvious notion was provided by the film actor Humphrey Bogart. It's both more churlish, and more honest, than the common view. **"The only reason to have money,"** said Bogart, **"is to tell any S.O.B. in the world to go to hell."**

chapter 4

Bloody
but Unbowed

War and the Military

ONE LITTLE MISHAP ...

A popular antinuke bumper sticker proclaims sardonically "**One nuclear bomb can ruin your whole day.**" It's interesting to discover that twenty-four centuries before the atom was harnessed, and almost two millennia before explosives of any kind were invented, a similar thought had been attributed to Thucydides. Born in Athens around 455 B.C., he was the father of what may truly be called history—as opposed to Herodotus's fantastic pastiches of rumor and myth—as well as a general in his city's long contest with rival Sparta. His vast *History of the Peloponnesian War* fuses respect for chronology and a fascination with human motives that make it the first classic of social science in the Western tradition. His two years of military leadership (424–422 B.C.) were not especially successful, however, and this may account for the subtle bitterness in the attributed line: "**One collision at sea can wreck a day.**"

. . .

DULCE, HELL

Among panegyrics to uncompromising patriotism, the most un-compromising may still be the Roman poet Horace's: ***Dulce et decorum est pro patria mori,*** or "**It is sweet and fitting to die for your country.**" The American Revolutionary spy Nathan Hale echoed the sentiment in his parting words "**I only regret I have but one life to lose for my country,**" and so have many imperiled warriors ever since. There have, however, been more jaundiced voices, among them one of this century's most vigorous and uncompromising warriors, U.S. General George S. Patton.

Viewers of the 1969 movie *Patton,* in which the general was bril-liantly portrayed by George C. Scott, will probably remember him as the tough guy who slapped a soldier recuperating from "battle fatigue" in an Italian hospital. The gesture, for which Patton later apologized, was characteristic in its outrageousness, for he was consistently intem-perate in his public pronouncements and as dramatically successful as they come on the field of battle. Whether it was in the Mediterranean, in France, or in the final push through a buckling Germany, Patton's shrewd command of U.S. tank forces was an indispensable element of the final Allied victory. He was good at war, and he savored its queer excitement.

Knowing battle, however, he did not romanticize it. World War I soldier poet Wilfrid Owen had amended Horace's equanimity in his bitter lyric "Dulce et Decorum Est," but Patton went the poet one further. "**The object of war,**" the tank commander once commented, "**is not to die for your country. It's to make the other poor bastard die for his.**"

NOT EXACTLY EDEN, WHAT?

If you want to write vividly, use concrete adjectives, they tell you in all the "How to Write Like a Pro" manuals. It's good advice, but there's always an exception that proves the rule. One of the most vivid adjectival strings in literature is composed of decidedly nonpictorial pearls. I'm referring to English philosopher Thomas Hobbes's description, in *Leviathan,* of the "state of nature" that supposedly preceded human society. In that state, Hobbes believed, bellicosity and its attendant, fear, were dominant conditions—the catchphrase for "Hobbesian nature" is **"bellum omnium contra omnes,"** that is, the war of all against all. Here's the kernel of his description of that state, with the pearls I mentioned bringing up the rear:

> In such condition, there is no place for Industry; because the fruit therof is uncertain: and consequently no Culture of the Earth, no Navigation, nor use of the commodities that may be imported by Sea; no commodious Building; no Instruments of moving, and removing such things as require much force; no Knowledge of the face of the Earth; no account of Time; no Arts; no Letters; no Society; and which is worst of all, continuall feare, and danger of violent death; **And the life of man, solitary, poore, nasty, brutish, and short.**

Not a picture in the bunch, but as a friend of mine says of cheap wine, "It does the job."

CLOSE CALLS

To my knowledge no soldier has ever spoken favorably about the experience of being hit by a shell. *Almost* being hit is another matter. Many veterans have spoken well of that, among them two future leaders of state.

As a lieutenant colonel in the British army in 1754, young George Washington was sent to the forks of the Ohio River, where both the British and the French wished to build a fort. An ensuing skirmish with French soldiers near Great Meadows, Pennsylvania, resulted in the death of ten Frenchmen, including their commander; it also started the French and Indian War. Washington, who in this engagement came under fire for the first time, wrote his mother about the experience: **"I heard the bullets whistle; and, believe me, there is something charming in the sound."**

Another young British officer, a century and a half later, echoed the sentiment. Winston Churchill had graduated in 1894 from the British military academy at Sandhurst and three years later was serving queen and country on the plains of India. His first field posting there was to the troubled northern province of Malakand, where native tribes were expressing their dissatisfaction with British imperialism. Churchill, whose literary aspirations were far greater than Washington's, wrote his first book, *The Story of the Malakand Field Force,* about the experience, and in that book he thus assesses the thrill of combat: "**Nothing is more exhilarating than to be shot at without result.**"

MAXIMS OF COMMAND

Of the many comments on the craft of war attributed to Corsica's "little colonel" Napoleon Bonaparte, many display the common sense that made him one of the two or three finest generals in history, while others reveal the vaingloriousness and pomposity that made him, outside of France, the most despised Frenchman in history before Charles de Gaulle. In Napoleon's mouth, logistical commonplaces achieved the rank of maxims: "**An army marches on its stomach**" and the less well-known "**War is made possible by biscuits.**" The military man's entrenched suspicion of public opinion became an adage that Richard Nixon might have endorsed: "**Four hostile newspapers are more to be feared than a thousand rapiers.**" Soldiers were described on the one hand as dispensable pawns ("**Soldiers are made to be killed**") and on the other as symbolic carriers of national pride ("**Every French soldier carries in his cartridge pouch a marshal's baton**").

One consistency in the Corsican's pronouncements was his self-esteem, linked throughout his career to military prowess. As the former emperor lay dying, he described himself not as the leader of France but as "**head of the army.**" "**I made all my generals out of mud,**" he is supposed to have said at one point, and it was a characteristic, even if apocryphal, observation. He knew, and he made sure that everyone else knew, who was in charge.

His self-esteem sometimes tipped over into an Achillean faith that he was invincible. Just months before his fall, he was asked whether he had ever been hit on the field of battle. He replied, "**The bullet that is to kill me has not been cast.**" He was right, too. He died of stomach cancer in exile on the island of St. Helena.

WINTER OF DISCONTENT

As Britain and France were facing off against Russia in the conflict that would become the Crimean War, Czar Nicholas I was quoted in the London humor magazine *Punch:* "**Russia has two generals whom she can trust: Generals January and February.**" Presumably, the magazine's editors wished to call attention to the shakiness in the Russian high command, but there was a positive angle as well to the czar's observation. He meant that the most reliable of his strategists was the Russian winter.

There was a precedent proving the wisdom of his words: Napoleon's fateful error, in the summer of 1812, to add Czarist Russia to his trophy shelf. In June approximately 450,000 of the French emperor's soldiers—his proud Grand Armée—crossed the Niemen River, chasing a retreating Russian force in the direction of Moscow. What followed was disaster. During the five months that the French were on Russian soil, although they never really lost a battle and they took Moscow itself without a fight, they were so battered by the premature onset of the Russian winter that their "victorious" invasion prompted Napoleon's fall. When the remnants of his starved and freezing force crossed the Berezina River out of Russia that November, fewer than ten thousand of the original horde were still able to fight. Had they stayed for Generals January and February, it's very likely there would have been none.

As for Nicholas's immediate cogency, the Crimea was much farther south than frigid Moscow, and weather played a minor role in ending that conflict. Peace negotiations did begin at the end of February, but they were brought on as much by Russia's fear of Austrian involvement as by the Allies' sufferings at the hands of steppe-born winds. It was a different story in the winter of 1942, when Adolf Hitler repeated Napoleon's mistake—and sent his eastern front troops to a similar fate.

GOOD OFFENCES MAKE GOOD NEIGHBORS

In 1844 an unknown Tennesseean named James K. Polk became
the Democratic Party's candidate for president on a platform that
promised the annexation of Texas. Such a move was bound to irritate
Mexico, which had lost Texas only eight years earlier, but it suited
a nationalistic *Lebensraum* mood that journalist John Soule called "Manifest Destiny," and Polk entered the White House in 1845. Within
months Texas came into the Union, Mexican troops clashed with
American forces near the Rio Grande, and the United States declared
war on its southern neighbor.

To those who agreed with Soule that Americans were destined
**"to overspread the continent allotted by Providence for the
free development of our yearly multiplying millions,"** the outcome of the war was gratifying. At the Treaty of Guadalupe Hidalgo,
Mexico gave up half a million square miles of new territory, including
not just Texas but also everything between it and California. The nation
hadn't acquired this much real estate since Mr. Jefferson's Louisiana
Purchase of 1803.

Abolitionists had resisted taking Texas on in the first place because
its settlers, largely southerners, permitted slavery; the Wilmot Proviso
of 1846 tried to block slavery from any lands acquired from Mexico,
but it failed on numerous occasions to pass the Congress. So Guadalupe
Hidalgo was no treat for antislavers. Nor did it please those who felt
that acquiring Texas was merely a pawn's move in the game of international expansion. Abraham Lincoln, opposed to the war on both
counts, voted for Wilmot dozens of times to no avail and needled the
expansionists with a memorable analogy. When fellow congressmen
denied that the conflict was a war of aggression, he likened them to "the
Illinois farmer" who had his own, private version of Manifest Destiny.
"I ain't greedy 'bout land," he proclaimed. **"I only want what
jines mine."**

. . .

THE MAGNIFICANT MUDDLE

In 1853 the sultan of Turkey, ruler of the unstable Ottoman
Empire, became alarmed when Nicholas I, the Russian czar, started
making moves on his northern borders. The czar's given reason for
his interest in Turkey was protection for the sultan's Christian subjects,
although the real reason, as everybody knew, was imperialist expan-
sionism. Nobody in Western Europe cared much what happened to
the sultan or his subjects, but to strategists, the Ottoman Empire—
affectionately known as the "Sick Man of Europe"—provided a valuable
buffer zone between Russia and the rest of Asia. To keep the czar's
grasping fingers away from India, the British were willing to back
beleaguered Turkey. France's ruler, Napoleon III, was happy to help
to divert attention from his own domestic troubles. The result was
the short but bloody Crimean War (1854–1856), named for the Russian
province where it was fought.

The war's most famous incident occurred on October 25, 1854,
as the Russian army attempted to drive the British out of the port city
of Balaklava. The Russians had taken a battery of Turkish artillery that
held the high ground along a narrow valley. The British command, eager
to retake this strategic position, sent in the Light Brigade of brigadier
general Lord Cardigan. Common sense would have dictated a flanking
attack, but Cardigan sent his men in head on, charging the guns in a
suicidal dash to glory and exposing them to a deadly crossfire upon
their return. Of the 673 cavalrymen who started the attack, 113 were
killed outright, another 134 were wounded, and because almost 500
horses were shot out from under their riders, fewer than 200 soldiers
could answer a regrouping muster. Military analysts uniformly depict
the affair as a combination of soldiers' gallantry and officers' incom-
petence.

The Charge of the Light Brigade survives in British folklore largely
because of Alfred Lord Tennyson's poem eulogizing the riders who were
sent fruitlessly into the "valley of death." The best on-the-spot summation came from French general Pierre Bosquet: "*C'est magnifique,
mais ce n'est pas la guerre.*" ("**It's magnificent, but it's not war.**")

DON'T LET GEORGE DO IT

Before finding Ulysses S. Grant to run his army, Lincoln had endured months of frustration with other commanding generals, beginning with the difficult and dilatory George McClellan. McClellan did the Union a great service in training the Army of the Potomac at the outbreak of war, but he was cautious to a fault and fatally prone to overestimating enemy strength. Repeatedly Lincoln begged him to take action, and repeatedly McClellan waited for better timing. The veiled antagonism between the two hampered the Union war effort for almost a year and a half and elicited a number of witty moans from Pennsylvania Avenue.

The most often repeated of Lincoln's barbs was the letter, written with a bitter tongue in cheek, that read, "**Dear General: If you do not want to use the army, I would like to borrow it for a few days.**" A lesser known, but equally sly, observation was this nudge in the ribs masquerading as a carte blanche: "**If at any time you feel able to take the offensive you are not restrained from doing so.**" And there was the summation which Lincoln gave to a close associate after removing McClellan from command of the army in November of 1862: "**He has got the slows. . . . He is an admirable engineer but he seems to have a special talent for the stationary engine.**"

Evidence suggests that the irritation between the two men was more than a little personal. On one occasion while McClellan was still in command, Lincoln called on him personally at his home, and McClellan exhibited his "slows" with remarkable discourtesy, asking to be excused from receiving his boss until the next day. On another occasion, in response to Lincoln's requests for detailed field reports, the general sent him a sarcastic telegram, asking for orders on what he was to do with six cows that his men had just captured from the Confederates. The President's response, just as sarcastic, was "**Milk them, George.**"

∎ ∎ ∎

SALUBRIOUS INFIRMITIES

Ulysses S. Grant was a shy, bland Midwesterner whom the Civil War transformed into a phenomenon. Never flamboyant and seldom flustered, he led the Union Army to victory over the more engaging Robert E. Lee by doing precisely what his predecessors had failed to do—compelling his men to fight with dogged tenacity. American folklore recalls his gruff directness in a series of one-liners reflecting his simple strategy. When a Confederate commander proposed a cease-fire during Grant's siege of his position, he issued the response that gave him the nickname "Unconditional Surrender" Grant: **"No terms except an unconditional and immediate surrender can be accepted. I propose to move immediately upon your works."** When he was dug in against seemingly immovable rebel forces near Washington, he announced, **"I propose to fight it out on this line if it takes all summer."** And when someone asked him to describe his plan for battle, he said simply, **"Find out where your enemy is. Get at him as soon as you can. Strike at him as hard as you can, and keep moving on."**

In spite of his successes, Grant was much abused by people who felt he bought his victories too dearly—and who objected to his well-known weakness for the bottle. On both counts his commander-in-chief snapped to his aid. Observing that when the general occupied a position, he **"seems to hang on to it as if he had inherited it,"** Lincoln threw back one demand for his removal in a seven-word classic: **"I cannot spare this man. He fights."** With regard to his drinking, the president was more elliptical. According to legend, when a temperance committee asked him to fire the bibulous general, he responded, **"I wish some of you would tell me what brand of whiskey Grant drinks. I would like to send a barrel of it to my other generals."**

The drinking quip was an echo of an earlier story, told of George II and James Wolfe, the English general who died while taking Quebec from the French. Told by detractors that Wolfe was mad, the king is supposed to have replied, **"Then I wish he'd bite some of my other generals."**

POLITESSE OBLIGE

The military salute probably derives from a quite functional medieval custom: two knights raising the visors of their battle helmets to identify themselves and to show they mean no harm. Today the custom has lost this utility and progressed (some would say degenerated) into a formal acknowledgment of military rank. The rule is simple: The junior party initiates the salute by touching his or her headgear, the superior acknowledges the sign of respect by "returning" the salute, and the junior party follows the senior's lead in snapping the hand downward. The observance of this or similar saluting conventions around the world provides daily symbolic support for the chain of command.

But what happens between two officers of equal rank? They salute each other simultaneously. But if you're a stickler for regulations, that common sense solution may not satisfy you. It didn't satisfy the member of General Ferdinand Foch's staff who asked him mischievously which person should initiate the salute when, *par example,* two colonels approach each other. The French general's response, I suggest, should be written into the rule books. The first to salute, he said, should be "**the polite one.**"

ONE ON GOD'S SIDE

In 1917, after running as a Republican from her home state of Montana, Jeannette Rankin (1880–1973) became the U.S. House of Representative's first female member. Four days later, along with dozens of her male colleagues, she voted against American entry into World War I. She later called this vote against what she considered a merchant's war "the most significant thing I ever did." It didn't sit well back in Montana, though, and she failed in a bid for reelection.

Rankin was nothing if not consistent. She spent the years between World War I and World War II working on a variety of feminist and pacifist causes, including the nobly quixotic Women's Peace Union, which wanted to outlaw war by constitutional amendment. Then, as Hitler was gobbling up Europe, she rode isolationist sentiment to a

second Congressional term. Unlike other isolationists, she stuck to her
no-guns policy even after Pearl Harbor, casting on December 8, 1941,
the Congress's single vote against retaliation. This abruptly ended her
second stay on the Hill. She could console herself, perhaps, with abo-
litionist Wendell Phillips's comment **"One on God's side is a majority."**

Consistently committed to a Gandhian vision of nonviolence (she
visited India seven times in later life), Rankin also opposed U.S. involvement in Korea and Vietnam. During the latter conflict her moral
example was so admired that the 1968 antiwar march on Washington
included a Jeannette Rankin Brigade. She explained her stand in a couple
of memorable nuggets. One was pragmatic and personal: **"As a woman,
I could not go to war, and I did not want to send anyone else."**
The other was quirkily philosophical and, for a pacifist, pretty funny:
"You can no more win a war than you can win an earthquake."
She died a month short of ninety-three, as her country was finally
withdrawing from Vietnam.

LA PLUS ÇA CHANGE...

Shambling, lariat-twirling Will Rogers (1879–1935) typified a popular American type of entertainer: the down-home, no-nonsense
"cracker-barrel philosopher." From Artemus Ward and Josh Billings
through Mark Twain and Mr. Dooley, the character's lineage stressed
common sense over "book-larning," and populist mother wit over the
prevarications of public officials. It also included a streak of world-weary
cynicism, exemplified by Twain's thoughts on "The Damned Human
Race" and by Mr. Dooley's spying of opportunism in every political act.
Among these unscrubbed soothsayers, war especially was subjected to
attack, as in Ward's announcement of his Civil War patriotism: **"I have
already given two cousins to the war and stand ready to sacrifice my wife's brother."** "Cowboy Philosopher" Rogers's contribution to the tradition appeared in his popular *Autobiography*. Having
seen a generation mown down by the mechanized slaughter of the War
to End War, he offered a barb that would have done Mark Twain proud:

"You can't say civilization don't advance . . . for in every war they kill you in a new way."

FOR GOD AND COUNTRY

When Pearl Harbor was attacked by Japanese planes on December 7, 1941, Howell Forgy was a navy chaplain assigned to the cruiser *New Orleans*. The contradictory nature of that assignment was memorably expressed in his reaction to the chaotic scene: **"Praise the Lord and pass the ammunition!"** Forgy's fellow sailors liked the line so well that it quickly became a service catchphrase. Set to music the following year by composer Frank Loesser, it remained a popular campaign tune throughout the war.

But the sentiment precedes World War II. It goes back at least to the English Civil War, when Roundheads and Cavaliers faced off to defend Parliament and Crown, respectively, as "spokesbody" for the English people. In that war Roundhead leader Oliver Cromwell, who later became Lord Protector, won a major victory against royalist forces at Marston Moor in 1644. Reflecting his pious Puritan sympathies, his battle cry that day was, **"Put your trust in God, my boys, and keep your powder dry."**

THE HERO IN SPITE OF HIMSELF

No politician knew how to make more out of an ingratiating smile and an air of insouciance than the junior senator from Massachusetts, John F. Kennedy. Perhaps because he knew this slyly shy role worked best for him or perhaps because he was genuinely self-effacing, JFK made surprisingly little political hay out of the episode that first brought him public attention: his heroism as the shipwrecked skipper of *PT–109*. When the torpedo boat was sliced in half by a Japanese destroyer in the summer of 1943, the young lieutenant got his crew to shore through shark-infested waters, towing one of them by gripping the crewman's life jacket between his teeth. Then he kept up their flagging spirits until rescue came, earning for his feat a Purple Heart and the Navy and Marine Corps Medal. An opportunist could have turned this business into thousands of votes, but Kennedy consistently played it down, both publicly and privately.

When writer Robert Donovan, for example, turned the episode into a book and then a movie, he did so with the grudging OK of the story's subject. When Edward R. Murrow asked him about the experience, Kennedy acknowledged only that it was "interesting." Most curtly, when a midwestern teenager asked him how he had become a war hero, he shrugged matter-of-factly, "**It was easy. They sank my boat.**"

WITH GOD ON OUR SIDE

In his account of the dark prelude to World War II, *The Gathering Storm,* Winston Churchill says that when French Premier Pierre Laval asked Joseph Stalin, around 1935, to ingratiate himself with the pope by encouraging Russian Catholicism, the Man of Steel sneered, "**How many divisions has the pope?**" Stalin seems to have liked the quip, for the same question was attributed to him on two other occasions, the 1945 Yalta and Potsdam conferences.

Dwight D. Eisenhower, referring to Yalta, told the *New York Times* on May 10, 1965, that Stalin's comment "shows us the Communist mentality clearly." True enough, although Ike might have recalled that a similarly jaundiced version of the "might makes right" philosophy had been expressed three centuries earlier by a non-Communist, and very Christian, French general. He was Henri de La Tour d'Auverge, Viscomte de Turenne, and for almost fifty years—until his death in battle at the age of sixty-three—he served the Bourbons against their colonial rivals, the Spanish and Dutch. Here's his comment on the moral aspects of the so-called Wars of Religion: "**God is always on the side of the big battalions.**"

SEWER SMARTS

Most encomiums for war come from troglodytic goose-steppers. One notable exception is found in *The Third Man,* British director Carol Reed's gloomy evocation of postwar Vienna, which was his country's critical and commercial success of 1949. The villain of that piece, Harry Lime, is (to quote screenwriter Graham Greene's own description) "a light, amusing, ruthless character" who has "never felt affection for anybody but himself." Since his business in Vienna is selling watered-down penicillin on the black market, he's certainly as amoral as any goose-stepper. But his ruthlessness has literary panache. To his old friend Holly Martins, he says flippantly,

In Italy for thirty years under the Borgias they had warfare, terror, murder, bloodshed. They produced Michelangelo, Leonardo da Vinci, and the Renaissance. In Switzerland they had brotherly love, five hundred years of democracy and peace, and what did that produce? The cuckoo clock.

This stirringly bitter speech was not in Graham Greene's original script. Orson Welles, who played Lime, wrote it in. The sentiments are not bought by Holly Martins (Joseph Cotton). When he discovers Lime's racket, he tracks him down in the city sewers and does him in.

WHAT PRICE VICTORY?

The word *victory* has acquired in this century a slight film of impropriety if not opprobrium, as if the "just war" were a thing of the past, or perhaps a tendentious conceit invented by rulers to secure support. Woodrow Wilson shocked the Congress and the nation in January of 1917 when he called for a "peace without victory"—that is, without humiliation of the losers—in the European War, but the idea was only shocking because it was new: In previous wars, humiliating the defeated had been part of the fun. Wilson's plea set a novel tone, and even though it was unheeded at the time, it has resurfaced in American history up to the present.

A kind of watershed in attitudes toward victory was reached in Korea, the first big test of the superpowers' Cold War rivalry. Douglas MacArthur, in command of U.S. ground forces, expressed the conventional view when he said, **"In war there is no substitute for vic-**

tory." President Truman, in removing him from command, hinted that victory at the price of global war might not be worth it, and subsequent leaders have tended to second Harry's moderation. Vietnam, many would say, was lost to the North Vietnamese because the United States would not buy victory at the price of holocaust. President Johnson himself, whom only the lunatic fringe could accuse of harboring dovelike sentiments, proclaimed in a 1964 speech, "**Victory is no longer a truth. It is only a word to describe who is left alive in the ruins.**" The Cold War trepidation evident in that statement kept people like Curtis ("**Bomb them back into the Stone Age**") LeMay out of the Southeast Asian driver's seat and reflected the political consensus that we'd better *look* for victory's substitute. Johnson's phrasing, incidentally, eerily prefigured that of a 1970s bumper sticker: "**War doesn't decide who's right—only who's left.**"

ETERNAL DODGE

If you doubt that the Western remains a vibrant influence on the emotional life of young Americans, consider its effect outside the cinemas, not within them. That effect remains tremendous, and it's not because of the current crop of oaters. Forget about *Young Guns* and TV's *Young Riders,* which are no more than cynical cash-ins on brat pack appeal. The Western's real impact on the American psyche was laid much earlier, with a hundred showdowns by Marshal Dillon in the streets of Dodge.

Proof? A week or so after the beginning of the brief, exultant Gulf War of 1991, a young U.S. serviceman was interviewed on CNN. How was the fighting going? he was asked. Great, he said. Coalition forces attacked, and Saddam Hussein's men ... well, "**They got out of Dodge.**" The speaker couldn't have been over twenty-five, and TV's *Gunsmoke,* where James Arness's Dillon cleaned up Dodge regularly for eighteen years, hasn't aired in prime-time since 1975. Either reruns are doing a hell of a job of programming a new generation, or there's a good case to be made for collective memory.

chapter 5

The Groaning Board

Food and Drink

YOU ARE WHAT YOU EAT

Anthelme Brillat-Savarin was the author of the West's first great gastronomic guide, *La Physiologie du goût* (The Physiology of Taste, 1825) and also of the gustatory proverb **"You are what you eat."** In French, the master's full comment was *"Dis-moi ce que tu manges et je dirai ce que tu es,"* or "Tell me what you eat and I'll tell you what you are." Vegetarians, taking that adage to heart, often argue that aggressive behavior would be reduced if we all chomped more radicchio and less red meat. It would be easier to credit this idea if Adolf Hitler hadn't been a vegetarian.

Yippie leader Abbie Hoffman, in his 1968 book *Revolution for the Hell of It,* gave the digestion-equals-disposition idea a grotesquely whimsical twist when he wrote, **"I believe in compulsory cannibalism. If people were forced to eat what they kill, there would be no more war."**

SOMETHING FISHY

Even the most devoted ichthyophile must acknowledge that, unless they are served absolutely fresh, fish have a nasty tendency to turn . . . well, nasty. The old quip about fish and guests smelling after three days, commonly attributed to Ben Franklin, is only the most famous of many laments regarding the unfortunately odiferous properties of the "briny tribe." If, like me, you feel that a good bluefish makes the tenderest steak seem like a punishment, you will be happy to know that there is a cure for this problem. The inventor was the radio comedian Fred Allen. **"How do you stop a dead fish from smelling?"** Allen asked. **"Simple. Cut off its nose."**

LESS RADICCHIO, MONSIEUR?

There's no question that *nouvelle cuisine,* that lean mean art developed in France in the late 1960s, is better for you than *vieille cuisine.* But there's nothing particularly *nouvelle* about it except the marketing savvy that sold it to yuppie Americans, at the beginning of Mr. Reagan's flash decade, as the latest gustatory find from holy France. Its components were simple: fresh ingredients, less fat, smaller servings, and artful arrangement. With the exception of the aesthetic element—a critical factor in marketing—there was nothing there that hadn't been pushed, ad nauseam, by lettuce nibblers for the previous twenty years. Take any back-to-the-land garden grubfest from the 1960s, cut the portions in half, and shuffle the remainder around your plate in a pentangle or triskelion pattern and—voilà! you've got *nouvelle cuisine.*

Because savvier cooks knew the fad to be much ado about less, they spent little time puckering up to Wolfgang Puck. Among these savvier souls, Julia Child said it best. As the American grande dame of French cooking, she didn't have to pucker up to anyone, and her regal confidence informed a sniffing assessment that she gave to the *San Francisco Chronicle* in 1982: **"It's so beautifully arranged, you know somebody's fingers have been all over it."** Her fellow TV cook

Jeff Smith (the *Frugal Gourmet*) agreed. Smith said, "**It's toy food. Feed it to toy people.**"

FOODS FOR THOUGHTLESSNESS

In his delightful compendium of American phrases *I Hear America Talking,* Stuart Berg Flexner cites Democratic politician Al Smith in a 1936 speech saying, "**No matter how thin you slice it, it's still baloney.**" Smith may have originated this gem, although he didn't originate the link between lunch meat and nonsense: *Baloney* had had that connotation since the 1920s, possibly as an Italian-American twist on the older *blarney.*

Spinach as a synonym for *nonsense* also originated in the 1920s, and this one is easier to pin down. It came from the caption to a 1928 *New Yorker* cartoon showing an unhappy diner presented with a plate of some unidentifiable vegetable. Informed that it's broccoli, he pushes it away, exclaiming, "**I say it's spinach and I say the hell with it.**" The cartoonist was Carl Rose; the probable caption writer was magazine regular E. B. White.

ROOT HOG—TO DIE FOR

What fungus has a "black, warty exterior," grows underground, and is accumulated with the help of rooting pigs? That's right, the truffle, and it doesn't sound too appetizing when you look at it this way, does it? No matter. The French will eat anything if it's weird enough and can be cooked in butter, and wealthy tourists, rooting for "authentic" fare, will eat anything if it's overpriced. Hence the truffle has remained a "delicacy" for many years.

Part of the truffle's appeal, evidently, is its alleged potency as an aphrodisiac. The great French chef Anthelme Brillat-Savarin (1755–1826) stopped short of making that claim for it, although he allowed that it was supposed to make women "affectionate" and men "amiable." This is odd because in the sixteenth century, according to the *Oxford English Dictionary,* the little devils were supposed to have the opposite effect: A

geography from 1591 assigns truffles the power to "subdue the flesh." I
don't know which myth the writer Colette had in mind when she gave
her opinion on the tasty morsels, but it's still the last word on their
attraction as emblems of excess: **"If I can't have too many truffles,"**
she said, **"then I'll do without truffles."** You hear the same sentiment
these days about Häagen-Dazs.

IT'S THE BERRIES

The average supermarket shopper today has more choices in the
fruit section alone than the Victorians had in an entire market. This is
very nice—the infinite choices of capitalism and all that—but sometimes
I yearn for slimmer pickings. That's why, when I've got to choose
between kiwis and kumquats, passion fruit and papayas, six kinds of
apples, three kinds of melons, and two luscious-looking Caribbean glob-
ules whose names I can't even pronounce, I let my mind fall back lazily
to William Butler. He was a sixteenth-century English cleric quoted in
Izaak Walton's *Compleat Angler* as giving the last word on the kind of
options that stymie me. To Butler, the noble strawberry was the cream
of the crop. Walton has him state it imperiously: **"Doubtless God
could have made a better berry. But doubtless God never did."**
I admire that kind of conviction—although I bet Butler never went
eye-to-eye with a passion fruit.

THE BIG CHEESE

Charles de Gaulle's period of greatest success as France's leader
came during his exile in England during World War II. When he returned
to Paris triumphant in October of 1945, he soon found that repairing
a war-ravaged country was more complicated than exhorting the troops
over the BBC. For the next two decades, he was never far from the
public eye, although his hegemony over the French people was seldom
unquestioned.

His difficulty in creating a solidly supported national policy plagued
him into the 1960s, but it was never more severe than in 1947, when
factionalism (not to mention fear of a Gaullist autocracy) fractured his

coalition, the Rassemblement du Peuple Français. Shortly after the RPF broke up, de Gaulle explained his problems in a striking metaphor. Recalling that the external danger of Nazism seemed a necessary ingredient in creating national purpose, he lamented humorously, "**How can anyone be expected to unite a country that produces 265 varieties of cheese?**"

NO TOT, NO TOTE

In recent years, U.S. orange juice suppliers have done a good job of convincing the American public that their product is basically sunshine in a glass. In doing so, they have, perhaps unwittingly, adopted an ad slogan that was popularized by Louis Vaudable back in the 1960s. "*Un repas sans de vin est comme un jour sans soleil*" is the original; the literal translation is "**A meal without wine is like a day without sunshine.**" This may or may not be true, and even if it is true, it does nothing for those who like the occasional downpour. The logic, however, is understandable. Monsieur Vaudable owned Maxim's Restaurant. Unless Maxim's follows different pricing procedures from every other restaurant you've ever drunk wine in, it makes its money not on the food, but on the bar bill. That being so, a meal without wine would also be a meal without a profit.

ISN'T THIS A 176 MAVRODAPHNE?

Athenaeus was a second-century Greek grammarian whose surviving work, *Deipnosophistai* (The Gastronomers), contains not only hundreds of quotations from otherwise unknown authors but also some of the first surviving recipes in Western culture. Like Plato's more famous work, the setting is a "symposium," or banquet, at which the guests engage in conversation over their meal. In Athenaeus's work, luckily, the topics of conversation include the food itself. As a result we have several cheesecake recipes that antedate the founding of New York by hundreds of years. We also have a line that is tailor-made for a snooty waiter. When someone at the banquet presents a container of chilled wine and boasts that it is sixteen years old, the guest Gnathaena responds drily, **"It is very small for its age."**

CHÂTEAU CHARLATAN

When you consider the level of pomposity that attends the quaffing of fermented grape juice in fancy restaurants, it's not hard to concur with one of my beer-chugging friends that **"oenophilia is a social disease."** With all the label gazing and cork sniffing, the bottle breathing and "legs" watching that go into an innocent glass of wine, the uninitiated may be forgiven for assuming that wine drinking is a subtle religious rite, whether or not the drinker is clerically garbed.

The worst of this récherché game is the sommelier's jargon—and its studied brutalization by novice imbibers. In the thirty years or so since I made Bacchus's acquaintance, I've had numerous potentially enjoyable wine tastings ruined by vintage-savvy first-sippers who believe that even the house plonk must be certified with sesquipedalian adjectives. Their assessments are typically balanced in both concept and grammar: "full bodied yet astringent," "floral but not too sweet," and so forth.

My friends and I for years have aped this formulizing with such assessments as "dry but wet" and "flinty yet lugubrious," but I confess that none of our jabs has matched James Thurber's. In his cartoon collection *Men, Women, and Dogs,* he shows a dinner party of four with glasses raised. As his wife smiles slyly and the guests betray an air of "Say what?" puzzlement, the host announces, **"It's a naïve domestic Burgundy without any breeding, but I think you'll be amused by its presumption."**

SINKING BY DEGREES

Not even the staunchest defender of the grape can reasonably deny that the negative influence of alcohol is a cumulative business. The party-goer whose first drink has no visible effect and whose second imparts a mere giddy sheen will discover inevitably, should he continue to imbibe at a steady clip, that by closing time his acuity and balance are jointly compromised, and that the crisp hopes of 8 P.M. have turned to slush. Shakespeare said it about "lechery," but it's also true of everything else: Liquor **"provokes the desire, but it takes away the performance."**

The bibulous Greeks were well aware of the sinking by degrees that even the best wine brings. The pre-Socratic philosopher Anacharsis noted the typical stages of the goblet game when he said, **"The vine brings three kinds of grapes: the first of pleasure, the next of intoxication, and the third of disgust."** The English writer Henry Vollam Morton, in his book *In the Steps of St. Paul,* gave a colorful twist to the "stages" idea in this snapshot of a drinker's bestiary: **"One drink of wine and you act like a monkey; two drinks, and you strut like a peacock; three drinks, and you roar like a lion; and four drinks—you behave like a pig."**

My favorite modern equivalent of this scenario relates to tequila. As southwestern drinkers have always known, and as Gotham yuppies are beginning to discover, the juice of the agave plant may be fermented in three stages. The weakest is milky pulque, the next strongest is mescal, and the true firewater is tequila itself. A Texas tee shirt revamps this common wisdom by describing the Four Stages of Tequila as follows: **"One drink: I'm rich. Two drinks: I'm good-looking. Three drinks: I'm bulletproof. Four drinks: I'm invisible."**

I DO NOT THINK THAT THEY WILL SING TO ME

T. S. Eliot's wan hero J. Alfred Prufrock is as hesitant as Hamlet and as nervous as a cat. In the 1917 poem where Prufrock burst upon the literary scene, his diffidence is frequently expressed in culinary images. There is talk of tea and cakes, of marmalade and ices, as visual reminders of his social impotence. Expressing his frustration at never quite being part of the party, Prufrock says **"I have measured out my life with coffee spoons."** Then, acknowledging his reluctance to put himself forward, he asks rhetorically, **"Do I dare to eat a**

peach?"—with the implied answer a chin-sucking no. In both images, we perceive the crippling effects of cosmic shyness—that endearing quality that misreaders of the poem take as a plus.

Peaches, like most fruits, have a sexual connotation that was certainly not lost on the poet. As for the coffee spoons, you can take that to mean either J. Alfred's "small bite" sensibility, or a reference to the time he's wasted in cafés. Either way, it's an apt metaphor to describe his sadly "stirred, not shaken" approach to the drafts of life.

A SMOKE AFTER DINNER

Renaissance-era Europeans, reacting to the introduction of tobacco from the New World, typically took it as manna from heaven. Medical opinion commonly attributed curative properties to the weed, and even those who believed it health-neutral were appreciative of its supposedly "calming" properties. King James I of England, whose overseas dominions included virtually all of the tobacco then being marketed, was violently opposed to its use—he objected to its "Stygian" stink—but his carping was a minority view. Most puffers endorsed the opinion of Robert Burton, who in *The Anatomy of Melancholy* wrote of **"divine, rare, excellent tobacco, which goes far beyond all the panaceas, potable gold and philosopher's stones, a sovereign remedy to all diseases."**

Remember this is the early seventeenth century. Today we know that inhaling the "divine" weed provides such "remedies" as emphysema, heart disease, and lung cancer. As a result, contemporary praise of smoking is less contrived. If you stand up for tobacco today, you're either a R. J. Reynolds stockholder, a masochist, or a shortsighted hedonist. Such a person, evidently, was Graham Lee Hemminger, who in a Penn State college humor magazine in 1915 penned an incomparable ode to the weed's allure. I convey the gem in toto from my dog-eared Bartlett for the delectation of my Camel-riding friends:

Tobacco is a dirty weed. I like it.
It satisfies no normal need. I like it.
It makes you thin, it makes you lean,
It takes the hair right off your bean.
It's the worst darn stuff I've ever seen.
I like it.

chapter 6

God's Country

America and Americans

AMERICA THE BOOBIFUL

Most Americans have trouble even imagining that democracy, or rule by the people, can have detractors. Yet a suspicion of what British statesman Edmund Burke called **"the great unwashed"** and H. L. Mencken called **"the booboisie"** has often informed conservative thinking in both England and America. It's also led to some telling redefinitions.

Thomas Jefferson based his faith in democracy on the conviction that all men were created equal. G. K. Chesterton amended that proposition, defining democracy as **"the belief that all men are interesting."** Thomas Hobbes in the seventeenth century and Lord Byron in the nineteenth played with the idea of rule by the "best," respectively calling democracy **"an aristocracy of orators"** and **"an aristocracy of blackguards."** Alert to the enormous influence of the popular press under a democratic system, Ralph Waldo Emerson said it was **"a government of bullies tempered by editors."** Focusing on the system's penchant for applauding the average, Elbert Hubbard called it **"the dwarf's paradise."** British Conservative Benjamin Disraeli, even more contemptuous, called it **"the fatal drollery."** But perhaps the most interesting insight came from the American poet and critic James Russell Lowell. Democracy, he pointed out, **"gives every man the right to be his own oppressor."**

THE QUOTE THAT WASN'T

It's conceivable that George Washington never told a lie, and even that as a child he owned a hatchet. But the story most often told about his childhood—the famous cherry tree tale—was a happy fiction invented after his death by an itinerant parson. His name was Mason Locke Weems, and he gave us not only the deathless quote **"I cannot tell a lie,"** but also the picture of young George hurling a silver dollar across the Rappahannock and of General George kneeling in the snow at Valley Forge.

These supposedly historical tableaux all appeared in Weems's *History of the Life, Death, Virtues, and Exploits of George Washington,* which was widely read throughout the nineteenth century and was largely responsible for creating a Washington "cult" that was not superseded until the martyrdom of Abraham Lincoln. The parson, who was a great hand with a moral, specialized in "instructive" histories of the great and the obscure. Among his other publications were numerous temperance tracts, lives of Ben Franklin and William Penn, and such self-improvement guides as *The Drunkard's Looking Glass* and *God's Revenge Against Murder.*

When Weems wasn't inventing folklore, he was hiking backwoods America for a Philadelphia bookseller, peddling his own books as well as countless Bibles. As a salesman, he could have tutored Og Mandino. One of his tricks was to stand outside a saloon, weaving and slobbering, until he was joined by real inebriates. As they gathered, expecting to share rounds of cider, Weems would pull out *The Drunkard's Looking Glass* and begin his spiel. He stayed on the road with this game for over two decades, until his death, still in harness, in 1825.

. . .

MR. JEFFERSON'S LOST CLAUSE

Thomas Jefferson's most famous piece of writing, the Declaration of Independence, was submitted first in draft form and revised by the Virginian's less literary colleagues, including Ben Franklin and John Adams. Among the clauses that the Continental Congress decided to ax was one suggesting that slavery be phased out. Five years after the adoption of the Declaration, Jefferson wrote in *Notes on Virginia* his most bitter comment on that institution: "**Indeed I tremble for my country when I reflect that God is just.**"

The third president's opposition to slavery was tempered, throughout his life, by his era's conventionally patronizing attitude toward blacks—he called them "inferior to the whites in the endowments both of body and mind"—and by his own self-interest. Himself a slaveholder, he freed his "chattel" only at his death.

THE GENERAL AND THE GADFLY

Charles Sumner, a prominent Massachusetts member of the Radical Republicans during Reconstruction, fought the Lincoln/Johnson conciliatory policy toward the beaten South, demanded immediate voting rights for freed slaves, and led the fight for Johnson's impeachment by the Senate. Never short on invective, he once referred to the beleaguered president as an "enormous criminal." Johnson's successor didn't fare any better in the senator's eyes. President Grant's practice of appointing his cronies to public office Sumner called "**a dropsical nepotism swollen to elephantiasis.**" The two men's clash over postwar claims against England fueled their mutual enmity, and this came to a head in 1870 over the administration's plans to annex the Dominican Republic.

Domestic disturbances on the Caribbean island provided a pretext for Grant's interest in "protecting" its citizens, although the promise of a naval base obviously influenced his magnanimity. Sumner, chairman of the Senate Foreign Relations committee, adamantly opposed annexation, predicting that a "dance of blood" would ensue if the United

States moved in. He succeeded in getting the Senate to block the project, but he lost the chairmanship, to White House cheering, as a result.

An accomplished orator and prolific writer whose works fill twenty volumes, Sumner irritated the Grant regime until the day of his death. After the nepotism charge, Grant is said never to have passed Sumner's house without shaking his fist. When a friend informed him that the Bay State gadfly was not a believer in the Bible, Grant vented his animosity with uncharacteristic wit. "**Of course not,**" he commented drily. "**He didn't write it.**"

THE OTHER GUY ALWAYS DREW FIRST

The Wild Bill Hickok familiar to most baby boomers is TV's buckskin charmer Guy Madison, rescuer of damsels in distress, smiling accompaniment to many a breakfast of milk and Corn Kix, indulgent recipient of Andy Devine's mock-desperate plea "**Wait for me, Wild Bill!**" The real James Butler Hickok was a flintier character. He had to be. Although he spent some time in his youth driving stagecoaches on the Oregon Trail and serving as a Union spy during the Civil War, he made his reputation as a frontier marshal or "town tamer," and flint was part of the job description.

Wild Bill's field of operations was lawless Kansas. He started out there in 1866 as marshal of Fort Riley. Three years later he cleaned up what has been described as the roughest of all Kansas cow towns, Hays City, and in 1871 he did the same for unruly Abilene, the principal railhead for Texas cattle on its way east. He didn't succeed in any of his three hotbeds without resorting to gunplay. Given his popularity as a subject of dime novels, the actual number of notches in his gun is virtually impossible to determine, although even the *Dictionary of American Biography,* which makes every attempt to minimize his deadliness, says his Colts stopped "several" men in Hays City alone.

All of his killings, according to legend, were in self-defense—an idea that Richard Armour, in a wonderful spoof, takes with a grain of salt. The spoof is his winking history of the United States: *It All Started with Columbus.* His assessment of Wild Bill is as follows: "**He is said**

never to have killed a man except in self-defense, but he was defending himself almost constantly." He did so successfully until 1876, when he was shot in the back by an envious range bum, Jack McCall.

PROFESSION: RENEGADE

Born in Indiana, Eugene V. Debs went to work for the railroads at fourteen, joined the Brotherhood of Locomotive Firemen while still a teenager, served in both city and state government, and then left a promising political career to do union work. In 1894, as founder of the American Railway Union, he led his members in the famous Pullman Strike, which was crushed by Grover Cleveland's federal troops and got Debs himself a six-month jail term. In jail he discovered socialism, and in 1900, 1904, 1908, and 1912, he was the Socialist party's candidate for the presidency, earning over nine hundred thousand votes in the last run. In the 1916 election, his energy was concentrated on resisting American entry into the—as he saw it—European "antilabor" conflict. This got him ten years for sedition in an Atlanta penitentiary, from which he mounted his fifth, and most successful, candidacy, taking almost a million votes away from GOP winner Warren Harding. Harding was impressed enough with public sentiment for the sixty-five-year-old agitator that he commuted his sentence in 1921.

Debs's life may not have been either happy or conventionally "patriotic," but it certainly was consistent. He himself summed it up eloquently in a 1917 speech in Ohio: "**While there is a lower class I am in it; while there is a criminal element I am of it; while there is a soul in prison, I am not free.**"

MAKING THE WORLD SAFE FOR DEMOCRACY

Until 1898 the United States of America was what today would be called a second-class power. The fifth U.S. president, James Monroe, had issued a famous doctrine in 1823 that on paper made the Western hemisphere an American preserve, but the international might of the nation was little felt there, and farther abroad the U.S. presence was virtually negligible. The Spanish American War changed this. The United States's opening card in the turn-of-the-century scramble for overseas "territories," it ended with an American victory over the Spanish empire and the acquisition of real estate in both hemispheres. After 1898, with Cuba, Hawaii, and the Philippines in its sphere of influence, the United States had become a world power.

With power came the obligation to "get involved," and this meant a steady broadening of American influence overseas, most notably in World War I and World War II. Isolationism, a major thread in American thinking up until World War I, was pretty much done in by 1917, and by the 1950s, with America and the Soviet Union trading bomb threats, it was clear that wherever the Russkies poked their noses, the land of the free was sure to poke its own.

Reactions to the nation's new role as one of the planet's policemen varied considerably. The Soviets and their allies, predictably, lumped the U.S.A. with the other "imperialist" powers, condemning every move as an attack on workers' rights. Superpatriots here took the opposite tack, proclaiming the obligation of God's people to export liberty. Somewhere between these two interpretations lay the bemused perspective of British historian Arnold Toynbee. In 1954, at the height of the Cold War, he acknowledged both the intrusiveness and the good intentions of U.S. policy. America, he said, was like "**a large, friendly dog in a very small room. Every time it wags its tail, it knocks over a chair.**" He might have observed that the Kremlin puppy was also afoot.

THERE *ARE* SIMPLE SOLUTIONS

Thomas Riley Marshall (1854–1925), governor of Indiana and Woodrow Wilson's vice-president, didn't enter politics until he was fifty-four years old. Between 1875, when he passed the Indiana bar, and 1908, when he became governor, he was a simple Hoosier lawyer, practicing quietly in Columbia City, teaching Sunday school, and earning the respect of his fellow citizens for his tolerance and humor. Those qualities brought him national attention as governor, and he brought them with him into the Senate when he presided there. The most famous quip he uttered as president of the Senate came during a 1917 debate over the country's needs. Forget roads, military expenditures, and tax reform, he suggested. **"What this country needs is a really good five-cent cigar."**

A progressive Democrat, Marshall also had a strain of sentimental conservatism in him, which made him see the "old ways" of doing things as the proper ways and fed his suspicion of radical reforms. Constitutionally a strict constructionist, he once complained, **"It's got so it is as easy to amend the Constitution of the United States as it used to be to draw a cork."** He was not wildly sympathetic to the New Woman either. His humorous *Recollections,* published in the year of his death, were offered to the public, as he said in the foreword, so that **"the Tired Business Man, the Unsuccessful Golfer and the Lonely Husband whose wife is out reforming the world may find therein a half hour's surcease from sorrow."**

CITIZEN SCARFACE

Prohibition, which ravaged the United States from 1919 to 1933, was good proof of William Blake's otherwise dubious notion that law itself generates crime. As soon as the Volstead Act made the sale and manufacture of alcoholic beverages illegal, what had been a haphazard and largely harmless diversion was transformed into a cutthroat enterprise—business with all the moral stops removed. This meant little on the backyard still and bathtub gin scale. On the national scale, it meant the rise of organized crime, and all the muscle and mindless fury which that entails.

The irony of the Roaring Twenties lay in just this viciousness. Had the populace at large not been eager to violate Volstead, Dutch Schultz and Alphonse Capone might never have prospered. As it was, disdain for the law—from the White House on down—made it possible for such gorillas to become folk heroes. They were doing, after all, only what the American dream promised: becoming rich by playing free enterprise for all it was worth.

At least one of the early mobsters consciously recognized this. **"Vote early and often,"** Capone said during one Chicago election—

signaling his willingness to play with the system, if not within it. When he was arrested for tax evasion, he waxed indignant, saying **"All I ever did was sell whiskey to our best people."** Disingenuous, maybe, but not far off the mark.

TRUTH TO TELL

Politicians are fond of accusing their opponents of deception; it is so much easier than identifying the principles upon which they disagree and then arguing from those principles toward practical solutions. Two modern instances of this easy out are furnished by Harry Truman and Adlai Stevenson.

Truman's was a spinoff on the saying that continues to be most closely attached to him: **"Give 'em hell, Harry."** It was first yelled approvingly from a campaign audience as Harry was raking his Republican foes over the coals, and the Truman camp picked it up as a battle cry. About it Harry himself later commented: **"I didn't give them hell. I just told the truth, and they *thought* it was hell."**

Stevenson's comment, rhetorically ingenious, as befits an "egghead's" pronouncements, came during one of his unsuccessful runs for the presidency against the GOP's winning ticket of Ike and Nixon. Acknowledging that the falsehood charge was being thrown around recklessly, he coyly suggested a simple "compromise": **"If the Republicans will stop telling lies about us, we will stop telling the truth about them."**

ALICE, SELDOM BLUE

Because she had an exceptionally sharp tongue, Washington socialite Alice Roosevelt Longworth (1884–1980) is often credited with a pointed description of Calvin Coolidge: **"He looks as if he was weaned on a pickle."** Actually, Mrs. Longworth got the remark from her doctor, who in turn had picked it up from another patient. It sounded like her kind of line, though, and so it stuck. It didn't hurt, of course, as she told *Newsweek* magazine in 1966, that she "repeated it to everyone I saw."

The daughter of Teddy Roosevelt and his first wife, Alice grew up in the public glow of his extraordinary career, adopting his humor, his independence, and his zest for action. When he entered the White House in 1901, "Princess Alice" became a second First Lady, both charming and scandalizing Washington society by gadding about with the Newport-based nouveau riche. Novelist Owen Wister once asked her father if he couldn't rein in her partying. TR responded, "**I can be president of the United States or I can control Alice. I cannot possibly do both.**" Probably he took a secret glee in her exhibitionism and would have loved her later characterization of herself as "**just one of the Roosevelt show-offs.**"

An avid follower of politics, she was married for twenty-five years to Nicholas Longworth, an Ohio congressman who was Speaker of the House for six years. Her opinions on politics—and everything else—were seldom honeyed. She publicly cursed Woodrow Wilson for pushing the League of Nations, called Warren G. Harding "just a slob," and imitated Eleanor Roosevelt, to general hilarity, at dozens of gatherings. Long after isolationism had become anachronistic, she was still denouncing the United Nations as a Soviet plaything and skewering those who disagreed with her in inimitable style. It was perfectly fitting that an embroidered pillow at her Washington residence bore the legend "**If you can't say anything nice about somebody . . . sit right here by me.**"

JFK GOES TO THE WALL

Of the two candidates for the American presidency in 1960, Richard Nixon was considered the heavy, the Boston towhead more congenial and accommodating. On domestic issues Kennedy certainly was more flexible than the warrior from Whittier, but internationally there was little difference between them. At the height of the Cold War, Democrats and Republicans agreed that America's role was to hold the line against communism, and JFK bought into that mission with as much fervor as Joe McCarthy or Tricky Dick. Where he differed from his GOP opponent was not in substance but in the famous "Kennedy style."

As president, Kennedy beefed up the U.S. presence in Southeast

Asia and mounted three other famous stands against the Red Menace. The first—a 1961 attempt to invade Fidel Castro's Cuba at the Bay of Pigs—was an unqualified disaster. In the second—the 1962 Missile Crisis—he went to the wall with Nikita Khrushchev, risking war to keep Soviet arms out of the Caribbean. The third stand—a literal trip to the Berlin Wall—was a public relations coup for the United States, even though it had no effect on the barrier itself, and even though the solidarity speech he delivered there contained a line that in anybody else's mouth would have elicited derision.

To confirm America's commitment to a united Berlin, Kennedy announced, *Ich bin ein Berliner.* The German crowd understood what he intended to say—"I am a citizen of Berlin"—and greeted the announcement with thunderous applause. But for the record that wasn't what his words meant. In German you don't use the definite article *ein* when indicating membership in a community or state; using the article changes the meaning entirely. What Kennedy should have said was *Ich bin Berliner.* What he did say was **"I am a jelly doughnut."**

ENIGMA IN DALLAS

John Fitzgerald Kennedy, the thirty-fifth president of the United States, died in a Dallas hospital on the afternoon of November 22, 1963, his head blown away by an assassin's bullet. At least a government investigation, made public in the Warren Commission Report, concluded that it was "an" assassin. The culprit, the report said, was Lee Harvey Oswald, a former Marine and Cuba sympathizer who killed Kennedy because of his unremitting antagonism to the Castro regime. The commission's "lone sniper" idea is still the official line, but no one who lived through the bitter backwash of the assassination can forget that the Warren explanation was only one theory among many. Numerous investigators were convinced then, and (as the popularity of Oliver Stone's movie *JFK* indicates) are still convinced now, that even if his bullet did down the president, Oswald did not act alone.

The difficulty of getting at the truth was compounded two days after the assassination, when suspect Oswald was himself shot to death, on live TV, by nightclub owner Jack Ruby—who subsequently, and some said conveniently, died in jail. Oswald never did admit his guilt, and many students of the case believed him innocent. Among them, not surprisingly, was his mother. Two weeks after Lee's death, Marguerite Oswald gave *Time* this curious explanation of why her "high-class" son could not have done the deed. "**If my son killed the president he would have said so. That's the way he was brought up.**"

THE BIGGER THEY ARE

Few American presidents had a more colossal ego than Lyndon Baines Johnson; none enjoyed playing the role of egoist more than he did. Lyndon knew he was a big man from a big state, and he milked the characterization, with all its theatrical possibilities, for all it was worth. What other president would have the vulgar panache to conduct press interviews from the toilet seat, or to display a gall bladder scar for the television cameras? It's as if, after decades of pressing the flesh and bulldogging colleagues, he had finally achieved the eminence he saw as his birthright and was determined to bask in the limelight, warts and all.

Before Vietnam, which he called "**that bitch of a war,**" skewed his perspective, LBJ handled the limelight well, frequently making fun of the very power he lustily wielded. On a visit to the LBJ ranch, German chancellor Ludwig Erhard is said to have remarked casually, "**I understand that you were born in a log cabin.**" Johnson came back spiritedly, "**No sir, I was born in a manger.**" Even more pointedly, on a stroll with his wife, Lady Bird, he is supposed to have asked her if she saw any Secret Service men or reporters in the vicinity. When she answered no, he replied, "**Then let's try that walking on top of the water again.**"

If Johnson was good at poking fun at himself, others occasionally got away with it too. Before Bill Moyers became a media star, he was first a Baptist preacher and then LBJ's press secretary. One day at lunch, it was Moyers's turn to say grace. With the piety of his original calling, he was mumbling something appropriate into the food when his boss yelled out, "Speak up, Bill! I can't hear a damn thing." Moyers calmly shot back, "**I wasn't addressing you, Mr. President.**"

MOON TALK

"**That's one small step for man, one giant leap for mankind.**" These were the first words spoken by astronaut Neil Armstrong when he left the descent ladder of the Apollo 11 lunar module on July 20, 1969, put his right boot in the Sea of Tranquility, and became the first human to set foot on the moon. NASA press releases later claimed he had actually said "a man," and that the article had been obscured by static, although Armstrong himself thought the "a" was simply "omitted." Article or no, I've always found the pronouncement pretty lame: sententious, falsely poetic, and clearly rehearsed. It's like the mission commander worked it over in his mind until he fashioned something that would quote well centuries on.

Probably I'd be easier on old Neil if *Apollo 11* hadn't already come up with a couple of unrehearsed, and truly poetic, transmissions. The very first words out of the *Eagle* from the moon were those of crew member Buzz Aldrin: "**Contact light**"—meaning an indicator light showed the module had touched down. Then, after a few technobabble exchanges about "mode control" and "command override," Armstrong officially informed Houston, "**Tranquility Base here. The *Eagle* has landed.**" Official jargon, both of them, but no lyric poet could have done better.

chapter 7

On
Stage

The Lively Arts

TRUST ME

It's a Hollywood cliché that, in a town where masquerade is the dominant industry, sincerity is about as common as Biafran blockbusters. The movie crowd comments constantly on this deficit, but few have put it better than comic Fred Allen. **"You can take all the sincerity in Hollywood,"** he said, **"place it in the navel of a fruit fly, and still have room enough for three caraway seeds and a producer's heart."**

Allen (whose original name was John F. Sullivan) was born in Cambridge, Massachusetts, in 1894, graced both the stage and movie sets in the 1920s, and achieved fame as a master quipster in the 1930s through his radio show "Town Hall Tonight." His phrasemaking ability is aptly suggested by the titles of the autobiographies he wrote before his death in 1956: *Treadmill to Oblivion* and *Much Ado About Me.*

THE BAD DREAM FACTORY

If you took all the poison ink that was spilled about Hollywood in its Golden Age and sent it to the set of *Cleopatra,* it might have floated the wily queen's barge, if not the picture. You could fill a book with Tinseltown *mal mots,* but let's settle for a handful of the most dyspeptic. Silent film star Lillian Gish called the place **"an emotional Detroit."** Her contemporary, H. L. Mencken's buddy and fellow balloon-pricker George Jean Nathan, thought it was **"the place bad guys go when they die"** and, more descriptively, **"ten million dollars' worth of intricate and highly ingenious machinery functioning elaborately to put skin on baloney."** The hypochondriacal composer Oscar Levant commented mordantly on the place's well-known pretentiousness: **"Strip away the phony tinsel and you can find the real tinsel underneath."** Finally, there was gossip columnist Walter Winchell, the frantically au courant Paul Harvey of his generation. To Winchell, Hollywood was **"a place where they shoot too many pictures and not enough actors."**

TAKE THAT, DAHLING

The Alabama-born actress Tallulah Bankhead (1903–1968) is remembered today largely for her husky throated rendition of the word *Dahling* and for her award-winning performance in Hitchcock's *Lifeboat* (1944). Because of her wit and racy behavior, she's also lionized, like Bette Davis, as a woman ahead of her time. Oddly enough, in her own day she was known as a fine stage actress, as popular in London's West End as on Broadway, whose triumphs included *The Little Foxes* (1939), *The Skin of Our Teeth* (1942), and *Private Lives* (1948).

Acclaimed as she was, she did once in a while pull a bad review. After one of these rare occurrences, she responded to the offending critic with a wonderful bread and rancid butter note. **"I am sitting in the smallest room in the house,"** the note read. **"Your review is before me. Soon it will be behind me."**

IN CHARGE

As a director, the British master of suspense Alfred Hitchcock was notorious for plotting out movies to the last detail, then leaving the set during the "boring" and "automatic" shooting stage. It's hardly surprising that someone with this limited sense of creative "inter-action" should have occasionally rattled the people with whom he worked. Actors in particular he considered little better than furniture, and his most famous remark reflects that opinion. "**Actors are cattle,**" he let drop one day in the middle of a film. Whereupon Carole Lombard stalked off the set and sent in her place a troop of oxen she had commandeered from a local farmer. Considering it politic to "apologize" to the press, Hitch told them, "**I didn't say actors were cattle. What I said was, actors should be** *treated* **like cattle.**"

The sense of control, both personal and professional, that this line implies also appears in a story about him causing a stir in a crowded elevator. Turning calmly to a friend, he muttered audibly, "**I didn't think the old man would bleed so much.**"

KING COHN

As head of Columbia Pictures in the 1930s, 1940s, and 1950s, Harry Cohn oversaw the production of Frank Capra's classic comedies and helped to develop both Rita Hayworth and William Holden. His reputation for creative insight, however, never quite matched that for tyrannical vulgarity. Under Cohn, actors were spied on, ingenues were routinely subjected to the "casting couch" test, and petulant tirades were standard operating procedure. Among the nicknames that indicated the esteem in which Cohn was held were "Harry the Horror," "The Meanest Man in Hollywood," and—writer Ben Hecht's contribution to the legend—"White Fang."

When Cohn died of heart disease in 1958, all of Hollywood turned out to see him off—one pundit said because they wanted to be sure he was really gone. Director Billy Wilder had a different explanation, what Orson Welles called "the greatest Hollywood one-liner ever made."

Why did so many former victims show up at the tyrant's funeral? Wilder mused: **"Well, give the people what they want."**

I HAVE IT ON THE TRIP OF MY TONGUE

Born in Warsaw in 1882, Hollywood producer Samuel Goldwyn dominated the silver screen during tinseltown's Golden Age, becoming the *G* in Metro-Goldwyn-Mayer and shepherding into America's movie houses such masterpieces as *Wuthering Heights* and the Oscar-winning *Best Years of Our Lives*. Aside from an obvious gift for putting together star packages (among his protégés were Susan Hayward, Gary Cooper, and Ronald Coleman), he was known for a thick Polish accent and a humorously adversarial relationship with the English language. About the numerous malapropisms that were laid at his door, he once said, "None of them are true. They're all made up by a bunch of comedians and pinned on me." *Echt* or not, they're too good not to repeat. Here, with a grain of salt, are my ten favorites:

1. **"I can answer you in two words: im possible."**

2. **"A verbal contract isn't worth the paper it's written on."**

3. **"Anyone who goes to a psychiatrist ought to have his head examined."**

4. To someone who had accused him of making a picture merely for money: **"I don't care if it makes a cent. I just want every man, woman, and child in America to see it."**

5. To an associate who argued against filming Lillian Hellman's *The Children's Hour* because it was about lesbians: **"Don't worry, we'll make them Americans."**

6. **"Our comedies are not to be laughed at."**

7. During the filming of a Western: **"We can get all the Indians we want at the reservoir."**

8. To a writer who asked whether Sam had finished reading his script: **"I read part of it all the way through."**

9. About criticism: **"It rolls off my back like a duck."**

10. His most famous line, upon leaving a meeting: **"Gentlemen, include me out."**

As Paul Boller points out in his debunking compendium *They Never Said It,* these gems originated not with "Mister Sam" but with various flacks and anonymous bon mot mongers.

FRANKLY, MY DEAR

The most famous line in the most famous movie in Hollywood history—Rhett Butler's farewell **"Frankly, my dear, I don't give a damn"**—cost its producer five thousand dollars. In 1939, when David O. Selznick was filming Margaret Mitchell's best-selling novel *Gone with the Wind,* the Hays Office was still very much in power, and Selznick was able to include the line—which millions of Americans already knew from reading the book—only after coughing up the modest sum as a fine. The Baroness Orczy speaks, in *The Scarlet Pimpernel,* of someone uttering "a good English damn," and I have the same affection for Rhett Butler's imprecation. You think the Axis would have taken American soldiering seriously if Clark Gable had said "Frankly, my dear, I don't give a darn"?

Rhett speaks the line to Scarlett O'Hara at the end of the movie as he is walking out, one last time, into the fog and she is whimpering that, without him, she'll be lost. By that point she has been mooning over Ashley Wilkes for three and a half hours, so by anybody's reckoning she's got it coming—whether Captain Butler, or the audience, cares or not. He goes, she cries, the curtain falls. And David Selznick takes the Oscar for best picture.

■ ■ ■

"TOTO, I'VE A FEELING WE'RE NOT IN KANSAS ANYMORE."

The year 1939 was a hell of a year for American movies. The coveted Oscar for best picture went of course to *Gone with the Wind*, but consider the nominees it edged out for the honor: *Dark Victory, Goodbye Mr. Chips, Love Affair, Mr. Smith Goes to Washington, Ninotchka, Of Mice and Men, Stagecoach, The Wizard of Oz,* and *Wuthering Heights*. Only Bette Davis's *Dark Victory* and Irene Dunne's *Love Affair* could reasonably be considered "merely" fine films, rushed into the limelight by their female leads' performances. Every one of the other films is a certifiable classic.

Of these stellar also rans, *The Wizard of Oz* has proved to be the most enduring. Thanks partly to Judy Garland's sensitively naïf performance as Dorothy Gale, partly to a richly talented supporting cast, and partly to a prize-winning (not to mention toe-tapping) musical score, the movie version of L. Frank Baum's story has become *the* American fairy tale, firmly embedded in our popular culture.

The movie is chock full of memorable lines, from E. Y. Harburg's Oscar-winning lyrics for Harold Arlen's "Over the Rainbow" to witch Margaret Hamilton's plaintive farewell **"I'm melting"** to Dorothy's return-to-Kansas formula: **"There's no place like home."** My favorite comes about twenty minutes into the action. After the cyclone sets the Gale house down on top of the Wicked Witch of the East, Dorothy and Toto emerge from the black-and-white of the opening scenes into the dazzling Technicolor of Oz, and the audience knows that *something* very wonderful is about to happen. Her comment to Toto pushes the plot magically forward.

"PLAY IT AGAIN, SAM."

As numerous trivia experts have pointed out, nowhere in the film *Casablanca* does anybody utter this line. In that classic schmalzfest of love versus honor, the first approximation of the line comes from Ilsa Lund (Ingrid Bergman) when she tells the café pianist (Dooley Wilson),

"Play it once, Sam, for old times' sake," and when he resists, repeats the request, "Play it, Sam." The idea is reprised later in the film, when her former lover, embittered café owner Rick Blaine (Humphrey Bogart), growls, "If she can stand it, I can. Play it!" But the "again" is a postfilm invention, known to stand-up comics and Woody Allen but not to Bogart.

The "it" here is Herman Hupfeld's exquisitely syrupy ballad "As Time Goes By." It had been "our song" to Ilsa and Rick in happier days, and it serves as a leitmotif for doomed romance throughout the film. You don't hear it much today unless you frequent piano bars, where it's as much a staple as "Misty" or "Over the Rainbow." The film's other musical hit, "Knock on Wood," has somehow gotten lost in time's shuffle.

Casablanca itself is still going strong. It won the Oscar for best picture, best director (Michael Curtiz), and best actor (guess who?), and as it approaches its fiftieth anniversary, it's still among the most popular American films of all time. Thank God Warner Brothers changed its mind about the leads. Their first choices were the stars of the previous year's *King's Row,* Ann Sheridan and Ronald Reagan. I guess I could see the versatile Sheridan as Ilsa Lund, but I don't even want to think about Ronald Reagan raising a glass and saying **"Here's looking at you, kid."**

THE CHANNING TOUCH

In Joseph Mankiewicz's 1950 character study *All About Eve,* Bette Davis plays Margo Channing, a fortyish dramatic star who is just having to come to terms with her age. Courted, flattered, and then insidiously pushed aside by ingenue Eve Harrington (Anne Baxter), she uses a brittle wit and an air of magnificent hauteur to maintain her authority as her audience turns to younger faces. The film's most quoted line, barked from a staircase podium, tells a cast party she is still a force to be reckoned with: **"Fasten your seat belts. It's going to be a bumpy night."**

Both Davis and Baxter, whose Eve is a precision study in honeyed poison, won Oscar nominations for their work in the Mankiewicz classic, although *Born Yesterday*'s Judy Holliday got the academy's nod. Director Mankiewicz, and the film itself, did win, as did George Sanders for his caustic critic, Addison De Witt. The film is also notable for the cameo appearance of a young Marilyn Monroe as a rising starlet and the critic's "protégée."

THE CONTENDER

On the Waterfront swept the Academy Awards for 1954: best picture, best director for Elia Kazan, best screenplay for Budd Schulberg, best actor for Marlon Brando, best supporting actress for Eva Marie Saint. The academy couldn't have chosen better. The Kazan/Schulberg story of Terry Malloy, a not-too-bright former boxer being used by a New York City rackets mob, demonstrated just how good the "social comment" film could get in the hands of moviemakers with critical intelligence as well as passion. One of the remarkable things about this "exposé" of waterfront corruption is that even the villains look like actual, complicated people. Mob boss Johnny Friendly is played with brittle charm by the incomparable Lee J. Cobb, while Terry's brother Charley (Rod Steiger) is fully rounded—a kind-hearted but venal study in imperfection who sees the tragedy of his criminal life but cannot escape it.

It is in a taxicab conversation between the brothers that Terry blurts out the pained realization that has become a set piece in Brando impersonations. Charley, Friendly's lackey, tries desperately to persuade his younger brother not to testify against him. When he pulls out a pistol, something cracks in Terry, and he realizes that, for all his ostensible affection, Charley has not had his best interests at heart. Reviewing his early boxing days, he recalls how the mob boss, with Charley's help, had persuaded him to throw fights he could have won. "You was my brother. You should of looked out for me. Instead of making me take them dives for the short-end money."

Charley protests that he was trying to keep him on Friendly's good side, and that he always laid bets in his name: "You saw some money." Terry moans, **"You don't understand. I could've been a contender. I could've had class and been somebody. Real class.**

Instead of a bum, let's face it, which is what I am." It's an enormously affecting speech, and it still works almost forty years later, no matter how often it's played for laughs by nightclub comics.

MIRANDA WHO?

There has always been a deep strain in the American consciousness of distrust for established authority—one might say, in fact, that the nation was founded on this sentiment. In every American simmers, just beneath the surface of statutory placidity, the soul of a raging vandal, a professional nose-thumber. This explains the immense and durable popularity of the revenge Western, in which a man frustrated by dilatory officials takes the law into his own hands, ridding the town of some black hat scum who was hiding in a loophole. It also explains the appeal of Clint Eastwood and Charles Bronson, whose most popular characters are revenant gunslingers, taming the city streets as the old-timers "cleaned up Dodge." The *Death Wish* and *Dirty Harry* series have the same message, ultimately, as *Shane:* If the law can't get the bad guys, do it yourself.

And do it with a sneer. The most popular line from the *Dirty Harry* series—so often quoted it has become a piece of folklore—succinctly expresses the bilious anger of the "good bad" crime fighter whose frustration leads him to bend, if not break, the law. The movie is *Sudden Impact* (1983). Dirty Harry Callahan, his .357 Magnum trained neatly on the small space between a criminal's eyes, dares him to make a play for his own weapon. "**Go ahead,**" he rasps delightedly. "**Make my day.**"

A DOG WITH SPOTS

After watching somewhere in the neighborhood of ten thousand movies no one else has ever heard of, I've reached the conclusion that the worst dog of all times still has, somewhere in its fetid innards, a redeeming line. Testing this theory on Howard Hughes's 1951 film *His Kind of Woman,* I find that even this canine clunker has its spots of light.

The cast includes Robert Mitchum as a dour gangster, Jane Russell,

Hughes's discovery, as an eye-batting gold digger, and Vincent Price as a fading cinema star. Two lines worth remembering: Mitchum says to Price, when asked how he liked the actor's last picture: **"It had a message no pigeon would carry."** And Russell says to Mitchum: **"They say you shot Fargo. How did it feel?"** Mitchum to Russell: **"He didn't say."** The writer of these memorable quips was Frank Fenton, who my Halliwell's *Filmgoer's Companion* tells me was a "general purpose supporting actor" in the forties and fifties. I would like to thank him, at this stretch of years, for his two sense.

A BON APPÉTIT FOR LIFE

The Hungarian-born photojournalist Andre Kertesz (1894–1985) had one of the longest and most productive careers in the history of his art. He taught himself the fundamentals as a teenager, moved to Paris in 1925, and there became a master of the small, hand-held cameras that were replacing the old box jobs as state of the art. In Paris and then in New York, he put in almost forty years on staff assignments for the glossies—*Town and Country, Look, House and Garden*—while transforming the stock requirements of such jobs with a keen sense both of humor and of design. When in the 1960s he finally turned to less commercial work a new generation took him to its own, and he became a star of the 1970s photography revival.

Indefatigable, Kertesz continued to work almost until the day of his death. Retrospectives crowded the last few years of his life, and the popular magazines rippled with interviews. When he turned ninety, still clicking, somebody asked him why he felt it necessary to keep working. With touching simplicity, he responded, **"I'm still hungry."**

MOTHERWIT

Anna Mary Robertson Moses (1860–1961), a New York state farmer's wife, turned to painting as a diversion when she was past seventy. Within a few years she was "discovered" by a Gotham art dealer, Otto Kallir, and skillfully packaged as a kind of "natural" Norman Rockwell. Rockwell's carefully crafted tableaux evoked an America where, as one

wag put it, **"nobody ever had to mail an alimony check."** Grandma
Moses's primitivist paintings served the same social purpose. At a time
of economic dislocation and war, they reminded Americans of the simple
memories that nothing could destroy . . . walks along country lanes, snow
on the meadow, the Christmas turkey. In Grandma Moses's world, as
in Rockwell's, yesterday was forever.

When she was past eighty, she got a state prize for her *Old Oaken
Bucket,* and she was intermittently lionized by, among others, Harry
Truman. But she never let it go to her head. Unlike a lot of canvas
dabbers with twice her talent and half her sense, she hadn't spent seven
decades slopping pigs and rocking young 'uns without figuring out who
she was or what things mattered. In the 1950s, when the kids in the
art schools were aping Jackson Pollock and gallery owners were learning
to babble in *ArtNews*Speak, somebody asked her what she "meant" with
her folksy landscapes. **"Painting's not important,"** she said. **"The
important thing is keeping busy."** Solid advice, which she followed
herself for 101 years.

THE DIVINE BEAST OF BAYREUTH

Few people are mildly neutral about Richard Wagner. An object
of both adulation and revulsion even in his own lifetime, he continues
to generate controversy a century after his death. His supporters maintain
that he fulfilled the promise of Romanticism with his impassioned,
elaborate stagings of Teutonic folklore. His enemies say he was out of
control both professionally and personally. To wit: His *Gesamtkunstwerken,*
or total theater works, were artistic monstrosities; his music makes
Beethoven's excesses sound like fast-food jingles; and to boot he was a
goddamned proto-Nazi.

You can argue the political implications of Wagnerism on your
own—not a bad idea in these days of resurgent *Deutschlichkeit.* As for
the music, I offer two swipes from nonmusicians (the professionals'
comments being about as clear as the Rhine at Rotterdam): The English
novelist Samuel Butler, comparing the bright humor of the Baroque
with the tortuous intensity of the fin de siècle, wrote in an essay on
Handel, **"If Bach wriggles, Wagner writhes."** And either Mark

Twain or the later humorist Bill Nye—the quote is attributed to both of them—said cryptically, "**Wagner's music is better than it sounds.**" I *think* he meant that you've got to admire the technical virtuosity of the Wagnerian process, but you wouldn't necessarily want it in your living room.

JUST THE BEGINNING

Al Jolson, né Asa Yoelson, was already one of America's most popular entertainers when Warner Brothers signed him to play Jakie Rabinowitz, a cantor's son turned vaudevillian, in the 1927 smash hit *The Jazz Singer*. Oddly enough, he was the studio's third choice. The original choice, comic Georgie Jessel, had balked during contract negotiations. His pal Eddie Cantor refused to replace him, and so Jolson, who had already sung a few tunes in Warners' experimental sound short *April Showers,* got to star in the industry's first sound feature. *The Jazz Singer* saved the ailing studio's bacon by pulling in 3.5 million dollars, made Jolson rich, and signaled the end of the silent film.

The film's most famous segment is probably Jolson's blackface rendition of the bouncy ballad "Mammy." Its most famous line is the star's jaunty acknowledgment of a vaudeville audience's applause: "**You ain't heard nothin' yet.**" This became a signature line for the forty-four-year-old singer and instantly became firmly ensconced in showbiz folklore. Club performers still sometimes quote it on their better nights, and it's been adapted by athletes and chefs as a promise of more to come: "You ain't seen nothin' yet" and "You ain't tasted nothin' yet."

TO EACH HIS OWN

By the early 1940s, Richard Rodgers (1902–1979) was an established Broadway tunesmith, the melodic half of the Rodgers and Hart combination that had produced the musical hits *Babes in Arms* and *Pal Joey*. Lyricist Oscar Hammerstein II (1895–1960) hadn't done badly either, with his credits including songs for the popular Hungarian operettist Sigmund Romberg and the book for the Jerome Kern smash *Show Boat*. When Lorenz Hart died in November of 1943, Broadway lost one phenomenal songwriting team but gained another, as Rodgers and Hammerstein began a partnership that ended only with the lyricist's death.

On their first shot out together, the duo came up with *Oklahoma!* (1943). Not bad for starters, and they followed it up, in quick succession, with *Carousel* (1945), *South Pacific* (1949), and *The King and I* (1951). With this string of hits behind them, Hammerstein was asked, in the mid-1950s, how they did it. Simple, he explained. "**I hand him a lyric and get out of his way.**" That formula worked for the dozens of now "old standard" songs in their 1940s shows, and it worked again in their last, great collaboration, the 1959 blockbuster *The Sound of Music*.

JAZZ IT UP A BIT, WILLYA?

Given the ludicrously high level of abstraction in most modern criticism of the arts, it's a treat occasionally to come across a professional review that you don't need a technical dictionary to understand. Case in point: Aaron Copland on Ralph Vaughan Williams. Vaughan Williams, perhaps the most famous classical composer that England produced in this century, introduced traditional folk strains into his compositions, much as Copland would later do in his *Appalachian Spring* and *Old American Songs*. No doubt to the untrained ear there are other similarities between the two men's work, but if so Copland glossed them over in a 1982 talk with the *San Francisco Chronicle*. There he told interviewer Herb Caen, "**Listening to the Fifth Symphony of Vaughan Williams is like staring at a cow for forty-five minutes.**" Puts me in mind of the "philistine" gallery goer who can't get anything out of Mark Rothko's blotches: "**I dunno if it's art or not,**" he says, "**but I know what I don't like.**"

HOUND DOG MAN

"Hound Dog" wasn't Elvis Presley's first national hit. That honor belonged to "Heartbreak Hotel," which topped the charts in the spring of 1956. That summer, his second winner, "I Want You, I Need You, I Love You," showed fans that the boy from Memphis could croon as well as screech, and marked his first step away from the rockabilly rawness that had sold Sun Records' Sam Phillips on his potential. "Hound Dog," backed by "Don't Be Cruel," was his third hit, carrying its dog-day raunch into the fall of that year. I was twelve, and for reasons that are not entirely clear to me, I remember "Hound Dog" as the initial Elvis monster—and, not so incidentally, as the beginning of rock 'n' roll.

This is not, I admit, acceptable history. Check any rock encyclopedia and you will find that Lloyd Price recorded "Lawdy Miss Clawdy" in 1954, that in the same year Bill Haley and the Comets covered Joe Turner's "Shake, Rattle, and Roll," and that in the following year Little Richard did "Tutti Frutti." So okay, Elvis didn't invent the sound. What he did was to drag it, kicking and screaming, out of the honky-tonks and straight into Ward and June's living room. Insofar as rock 'n' roll is inescapably media fed and middle class, that gives him a better claim to the "king" tag than anyone else. By the time he whumped out the immortal dumb line **"You ain't nothin' but a hound dog,"** you knew that rock 'n' roll as a national phenomenon was on its way.

As with most of his songs, the line wasn't his. "Hound Dog," first recorded by Big Mama Thornton in 1953, was written by Jerry Leiber and Mike Stoller, who for the Drifters wrote such classic 1950s tunes as "There Goes My Baby," "Save the Last Dance for Me," "Up on the Roof," and "On Broadway."

A CERTAIN JAZZ *NE SAIS QUOI*

Back in the early 1960s my friend Joel and I used to visit the old Five Spot, a Manhattan jazz club, to hear such legends as Coleman Hawkins and Thelonious Monk. One morning after a particularly inspired Monk set, we read a *Village Voice* review that talked about "unique harmonic inventiveness" and "experimental tonalities." If you say so. The on-the-spot review we got the night before was much clearer. It came from an old guy at the bar—stingy brim, shades, dangling cigarette—who sized up our college-boy naïveté, grinned back at our "Oh wow" expressions, and eased out, ever so conspiratorially, **"Monk is deep."**

That's the best embracive comment on jazz I've ever heard. The best abrasive one came from Louis Armstrong. Somebody even more naïve than Joel and me once asked him how he would "define" jazz for the nonaficionado. Satchmo growled, **"If you've got to ask, you'll never know."**

THE HARDER THEY FALL

If you're under forty or so, you probably associate this phrase with Jimmie Cliff, the reggae singer whose Jamaican-set movie *The Harder They Come,* with its expressive title song, lit up the college campuses in the early 1970s. If you're a little older, you may recall a cadaverous Humphrey Bogart, playing a disillusioned sportswriter, wincing his way through *The Harder They Fall,* his last movie before he succumbed to cancer in 1957. But before either Bogart or Cliff there was boxer Bob Fitzsimmons. It was he who coined the aphorism, **"The bigger they come, the harder they fall."**

Robert Fitzsimmons, born in Cornwall, began his ring career in New Zealand by knocking out four men in one night. He came to the United States in 1890, became world middleweight champion the following year by beating Jack Dempsey (not *the* Jack Dempsey), and took the heavyweight crown from Gentleman Jim Corbett with a fourteenth-round knockout in 1897. At six feet and 170 pounds, Fitzsimmons was a stringbean for a heavyweight, and he lost the title to bruiser Jim Jeffries only a couple of years after taking it from Corbett. It was before a 1902 rematch with Jeffries that somebody commented on the weight differential: Jeffries had him by at least forty pounds. Fitzsimmons's famous response proved to be a miscalculation. He never did retake the heavyweight title, although he held on to the middleweight one until he retired. That was in 1905, after a six-round scrapfest with K. O. Sweeney. Battling Bob at the time was fifty-two.

THE GREATEST

Muhammad Ali may or may not have been, as he frequently informed us, the greatest fighter who ever lived. He was certainly among the loudest and wittiest. From the time he won the national Golden Gloves title as a teenager to the day he bowed out of the ring twenty years later, Ali delighted his many fans with a stream of one-liners, theatrical boasts, and bad puns that upgraded boxing from a gutter game into a smart set diversion. By the time the Louisville whirlwind got done with the press boys, people who didn't know a cauliflower ear from a broccoli casserole had become sweet science aficionados.

Ali's chief attraction, aside from his mouth, was a phenomenally active ring style—a combination of tireless "rope-a-dope" footwork and a left jab that had to be seen to be believed. The speed in both those techniques was what he himself recognized as his strongest asset, and he immortalized it in his most famous line. When, early in his remarkable career, he was asked to define his ring strategy, he replied, "**Float like a butterfly, sting like a bee.**" For the years of his prime, that description was just as accurate as it was colorful.

chapter 8

Scribbler Wisdom

Writers and Writing

EVERYTHING ELSE IS POSTSCRIPT

When I was a child, my best friend was another future writer, Sandy Sidar. He went away to prep school when he was fourteen, and we traded pontifications about T. S. Eliot on summer vacations. Then we both went away—colleges, grad schools, different continents—and there was a gap of about a dozen years when our contact wound down to nothing, not even postcards. When we reconnected in our early thirties, I was astonished at how well we still clicked. Sandy had a disarming explanation. **"I figure nobody changes much after twelve."**

After cogitating over this insight for fifteen years, and being about to celebrate forty years of friendship with the guy, I've decided there might be something to his theory. It was a pleasure for me, therefore, to discover that Ignazio Silone, the author of *Bread and Wine,* made a similar comment to Murray Kempton in the 1960s. In his book *America Comes of Middle Age,* Kempton quotes the Italian novelist as saying, **"No one can ever write about anything that happened to him after he was twelve years old."**

THE ONE MORE TRAVELED BY

Sandy is also the guy who, when we were starting out together in the scribbler's trade, said there were two ways to approach the writing game. One he called **"Instant Eliot or Bust,"** which meant that you wrote only what you knew was truly in Your Heart of Hearts, perfecting your craft, polishing that *mot juste* over and over, even if it meant a diet of beer and mayonnaise sandwiches. This "suffer for your art" approach was the one we had both been sold on in college, and the one that most True Artists, according to the myth, are willing to starve for. Its disadvantage is that you—and your family—may very well starve for it (bet you Nora Joyce ate her share of mayonnaise). The advantage is that you don't leave crap behind.

The other approach Sandy called the **"Cheating Apprentice."** Here you write whatever you must to pay the bills, trying to pick up enough craft along the way so that when you win the lottery or run across Steven Spielberg at a party, you can pop up brightly and say "I've got this idea." The disadvantage here is that you leave garbage behind you, like a pack rat who feathers his nest with the world's debris. The advantage is that you and the family don't go hungry.

Prepublished authors all believe in the former path to immortality. Working writers all believe in the latter. So if you're a young word spark on the make and you know you're cheating your muse, don't despair. Console yourself with the olympian assessment of Doctor Johnson. In the spring of 1776, he told Boswell, **"No man but a blockhead ever wrote except for money."**

TRUE-TO-LIE EXPERIENCE

Do you have to "live fully" in order to write? Or can you sit down at your writing desk and just imagine? Do you have to be there, or can you make it up? It depends, of course, on what you write about, and the history of literature has plenty of examples to push both theories, the extremes being I suppose the Belle of Amherst, Emily Dickinson, for the "think about it" school, and Ernest Hemingway, the intellectual's

Rambo, for the "just do it" approach. Since Hemingway has cast a longer shadow over American writers than anybody since Herman Melville, there is no shortage of folks to rally to his example. Being shy of Pamplona scars and elephant-shooting medals myself, let me rack up a couple of points for the other side.

First is Thoreau. At the opening of *Walden*, he boasts, "**I have traveled a good deal in Concord.**" Later, he advises the reader, "**Explore your own higher latitudes ... It is not worth the while to go around the world to count the cats in Zanzibar.**" Second, a writer not unacquainted with the "experience" route, Henry Miller. Writing in *Sunday After the War* (1944), he suggests that writing of any kind may be sublimation: "**No man would set a word down on paper if he had the courage to live out what he believed in.**" Makes you think what Hemingway might have pulled off if he'd skipped the bulls.

The greatest fudge of this debate I've ever heard came a couple of years ago from Stephen King. When a goggle-eyed fan, amazed at his cleverness, asked him where he got his ideas, he responded without batting an eye, "**Utica, New York.**"

WHEN TELEGRAMS WERE A HUNDRED FRANCS A WORD

Thanks to Broadway, the pathetic fate of Jean Valjean, the protagonist of Victor Hugo's *Les Miserables,* has now been wept over by thousands of solid citizens who would happily have doubled his jail time if he stole *their* bread. The irony would not have been lost on the story's humanitarian author, since he witnessed a similar surge of crocodile tears in 1862, when the novel first hit the Paris bookstalls. Sales were so brisk that they occasioned a memorable wire exchange between author and publisher. Curious about the initial figures, Hugo cabled simply: "**?**" His publisher cabled back: "**!**"

. . .

GUESS WHO'S COMING TO DINNER?

Like Casanova, the Irish-American novelist Frank Harris (1856–1931) created his own reputation for lubricity, which then overshadowed whatever other gifts he might have had. In Casanova's case, the gifts were significant. Among his literary ventures beyond his scandalous memoirs were opera libretti, translations from the Greek, and a visionary novel. In Harris's case the gifts were more constrained, but owing to the marketability of cheap thrills in our century, his notoriety almost outstripped Casanova's.

Not that he lacked either talent or energy. Turning down a scholarship to Cambridge at the age of fifteen, he emigrated to the United States the same year, where he worked as a cowhand and earned a law degree from the University of Kansas before returning to England just in time for the Yellow Nineties. There he edited the influential *Saturday Review,* wrote a biography of Oscar Wilde, and established himself as a fringe companion of the London aesthetes. His kiss-and-tell biography *My Life and Loves,* rejected by English-language publishers on both sides of the big pond, came out under a German imprint in the 1920s.

Whatever his literary skills, no one liked him personally. Leaving no stone unthrown, the biographical sketch in *Twentieth-Century Authors* calls him "utterly devoid of humor, envious, malicious, bombastic, violent, prejudiced, and seemingly offensive on principle." It was this last characteristic, no doubt, that made him such a hit at dinner parties and that inspired Oscar Wilde's noted summary of his social career: **"Frank Harris is invited to all the great houses in London—once."**

A CHOICE OF NIGHTMARES

Like most ostensible socialists, George Bernard Shaw had no greater respect for the mass of humanity than your average Tory hack or royalist social climber. Much of his writing, indeed, seethes with a gleeful contempt for human nature, so that one expects he donned his Fabian coat for the same reason that Winston Churchill bore democracy: Threadbare as it was, it was still the best our execrable species could put together.

Churchill came right out and said it, when he observed, "**Democracy is a very bad form of government—except for all others that have been tried from time to time.**" Shaw, never comfortable speaking without a mask, put a similar thought among his "Maxims for Revolutionaries," part of the interlude feast in his play *Man and Superman*. In Shaw's phrasing, there's no winning either way: "**Democracy substitutes election by the incompetent many for appointment by the corrupt few.**"

BRIEF ENCOUNTER

Neither Edna Ferber nor Noël Coward were bona fide charter members of New York's famed Algonquin Round Table, so we must take it as singularly propitious that one of their encounters at the Gotham salon produced an exchange that was worthy of recollection.

Ferber (1887–1968), the older and more down-to-earth of the two, was a Midwesterner whose novels and plays depicted the diversity of the American middle class. She won the Pulitzer in 1924 for her novel *So Big,* did the books on which Hollywood based *Show Boat* and *Giant,* and with George S. Kaufman, an Algonquin regular, wrote the Broadway hits *Dinner at Eight* and *The Royal Family.* Coward (1899–1973), twelve years her junior, was the boy wonder of the British stage, as adept at stage management and acting as he was at writing such elegantly frothy comedies as *Hay Fever, Private Lives,* and *Blithe Spirit.*

Coward was also as wispily mannered in dress and bearing as Ferber was direct and robust. Partial to tailored suits, she sailed into the Algonquin one day to find Coward dressed in a suit similar to her own. He appraised her: "**You look almost like a man.**" Unblinking, Ferber replied, "**So do you.**"

. . .

GIN AND TOWEL, ANYONE?

A man climbs out of a cab into a pouring rain. Followed by dripping friends, he reaches the door of his apartment house, pushes it open, shakes himself off in the lobby, and says, **"Let's get out of these wet clothes and into a dry martini."** One of the great "Thank God we're home" lines, it's been attributed to both Alexander Woollcott and Robert Benchley. The odds are good it became part of drinking lore in one of the sodden meetings of the Algonquin Round Table. Woollcott and Benchley both hung out there in the 1920s, and both were known to tip a glass or two.

Woollcott, host of the popular "Town Crier" radio show, was also the model for the outrageous egotist Sheridan Whiteside in the Kaufman/ Hart comedy *The Man Who Came to Dinner*. Benchley specialized in dramatizing the myriad small indignities of modern life in such works as the book *From Bed to Worse* and the mock instructional film *How to Sleep*.

NOW YOU PLAY STRAIGHT MAN, MARC

The American playwrights Marc Connelly and George S. Kaufman both hit their strides in the 1930s, Connelly with his Pulitzer prize-winning play *The Green Pastures* (1930), Kaufman with the Hart/Kaufman treasures *You Can't Take It with You* (1936) and *The Man Who Came to Dinner* (1939). Before hooking up with Moss Hart, however, Kaufman had collaborated frequently with Connelly, notably on *Merton of the Movies* (1922) and *Beggar on Horseback* (1924). The two friends also hung around the Algonquin together, and their association occasioned a classic ribald exchange regarding Connelly's premature baldness. Kaufman, with mock condescension, said, **"I like your bald head, Marc. It feels just like my wife's behind."** Connelly rubbed his hand slowly over his head, looked thoughtful, and replied, **"So it does, George, so it does."**

. . .

FIT AUDIENCE THOUGH NONE

I believe that there are certain famous books that no one, not even professors who teach them, has ever actually read. *Moby Dick,* for example. Sure, we all boned up on the rope-coiling and blubber-boiling bits in high school so our teachers would think we'd read every word, but do you know anybody who actually did? Proust's *Remembrance* fits into the same category. Marx's *Das Kapital.* And—I say this without an instant's hesitation—James Joyce's *Finnegan's Wake.* People read the book's skeleton key, yes, but the monster itself? As the Italians say, "Don't make me illusions."

Joyce expressed the obvious reason himself when he moaned self-pityingly, "**Does nobody understand?**" The answer to that question is also obvious—"Not when you write like this, Bubba"—but Joyce framed it, unfortunately, when it was too late to do anything about it. He was dying at the time, and this bleak mouthing was his last reported utterance. Notice the construction. Even in extremis, any normal person would have asked, "Doesn't anybody understand?"—hinting that he wishes they would. Joyce's grammatical weirdness implies that he was *hoping* nobody would understand.

DON'T APPLAUD, JUST THROW MONEY

Erle Stanley Gardner, the lawyer-writer who created Perry Mason, was among the most prolific and successful authors of this century. After introducing his famous sleuth in his first book, *The Case of the Velvet Claws* (1933), Gardner produced dozens of other Mason volumes, more than twenty books under the pseudonym A. A. Fair, and countless short stories and novelettes. Before he died in 1970 at the age of eighty, he had turned out more than a hundred volumes, become the most widely translated of all American authors, and seen Raymond Burr turn his fictional creation into a fixture of American popular culture.

Gardner once explained Mason's popularity as a lust in the common man for a sense of justice. "Since prohibition, since rationing in World War II, since the income tax, the average man goes around with a vague sense of uneasiness. He wants to be reassured that there is an advocate who will defend him and get him off. Perry Mason is that kind of lawyer." Someone who displays this canny sense of his own audience might be forgiven the occasional lapse of modesty—even if he hadn't sold 165 million copies. Such a lapse occurred late in the great man's career, when he sent a manuscript to a picky editor with the following note: **"It's a damn good story. If you have any comments, write them on the back of a check."**

IT'S ALL PACKAGING, YOU KNOW

Whatever you think of his plots, you've got to admit that Somerset Maugham (1874–1965) was a great hand with a title. Take only a quartet of his most successful books: *Of Human Bondage, Cakes and Ale, The Moon and Sixpence, The Razor's Edge*. Bookstore lodestones, every one. I won't go so far as to say that Maugham's success was built on his skill at title creation, but that skill certainly didn't hurt. How many copies do you suppose *Bondage* would have sold if he'd called it *How I Got to Be a Country Doctor?*

I'm not the first person to have recognized this. James Humes, in his charming social climber's guide *How to Get Invited to the White House* (1977), recounts the story of an aspiring author who came to Maugham for advice. He'd written a book, but was blocked on the title. How did Maugham come up with such wonderful titles for *his* books? And would he mind very much reading the magnum opus and offering suggestions?

No need to read it, said Maugham. "Just tell me. Does it have anything about drums in it?"

No, responded the young writer. Nothing about drums.

"What about bugles? Anything in it about bugles?"

No again. Not a single bugle.

"Fine, then," concluded Maugham. **"I suggest that you call it *No Drums, No Bugles.*"**

THE SMALLER THE TARGET, THE BETTER

As a rule, writers prefer silence to laughter. If your work is ignored, you can console yourself with the promise of posterity. If it's ridiculed, you have to be a pretty strong cookie not to retreat, whining, "They just don't *understand.*" And, because for every writer who's trying to do decent work and shut up about it, there is at least one reviewer who cannot sleep at night without a blood nightcap, risibility is the bête noire of the scribbling tribe. That's why Ernest Hemingway's statement in the *Paris Review,* made three years before he ended his life, should be emblazoned above every would-be author's desk: "**The most essential gift for a writer is a built-in, shockproof shit-detector. This is the writer's radar and all great writers have it.**" The idea being that, if you can catch your own shit before it becomes a "text," the lit-crit crowd won't get to push your nose in it. William Kennedy, the upstate New York literary "find" of the 1980s, may have had this in mind when, reflecting on the fragility of his craft, he commented, "**There's only a short walk from the hallelujah to the hoot.**"

AND YOUR POETRY STINKS TOO

Edmund Wilson (1895–1972) went to Princeton with F. Scott Fitzgerald; Carl Sandburg (1878–1967) dropped out of school at thirteen, hoboed around the country, and worked his way through tiny Lombard College. Wilson was New York City and aggressively cosmopolitan; Sandburg was Chicago, down-home, and just as aggressively American. Wilson's attitude toward the Civil War is suggested by his book on that conflict's literature, *Patriotic Gore;* Sandburg won his first Pulitzer prize for an adulatory biography of war leader Lincoln.

With these differences, it's hardly to be expected that critic Wilson would be ready with garlands for Sandburg's work. He wasn't. When the Chicago bard's Lincoln biography came out, Wilson was among the three or four people in the country who didn't think it was the greatest thing since sliced bread. In *Time* magazine, he gave this estimation: "**The cruelest thing that has happened to Lin-**

coln since being shot by Booth was to have fallen into the hands of Carl Sandburg."

STREAM OF UNCONSCIOUSNESS

Most writers agree that good writing is the product of endless revision. **"All writing is rewriting,"** goes a common trade adage, and Elmore Leonard has amended this to humorous effect. Explaining the terse, painstakingly "natural" style of his mysteries, he says, **"If it sounds like writing, I rewrite it."**

Among those who publicly rejected this common wisdom was the Beat poet and novelist Jack Kerouac. Subscribing to the same fallacy that compels teenaged poets to confuse lack of discrimination with "honesty," he once confessed that he *never* revised what he wrote: As it came out of the typewriter, so it stayed. Personally, I find this hard to believe, but if it's true, it would certainly explain the ragbag quality of his *Mexico City Blues*.

To the creatively lethargic, Kerouac's boast might appear to be evidence of natural genius. Truman Capote knew better. Reacting to the self-congratulatory admission, he is reputed to have said, **"That's not writing, it's typing."**

WHAT DID YOU SAY THE TOWER SYMBOLIZED, AGAIN?

Writers constantly complain about the critic's propensity to rip apart what he doesn't understand, and anyone who has had a favorite poem "analyzed" into smithereens will sympathize with the Blakean assessment of the critical faculty: **"We murder to dissect."** That's as economic a dismissal of the meddling mind as you are likely to find. A longer and more colorful one is found in J. R. R. Tolkien's 1936 essay "The Monster and the Critics." He is speaking of his fellow professors' reducing *Beowulf* to rubble by what today would be called "contextualization." The passage, which works by way of a vivid analogy, is too striking not to quote in full:

A man inherited a field in which was an accumulation of old stone, part of an older hall. Of the old stone some had already been used in building the house in which he actually lived, not far from the old house of his fathers. Of the rest he took some and built a tower. But his friends coming perceived at once (without troubling to climb the steps) that these stones had formerly belonged to a more ancient building. So they pushed the tower over, with no little labor, in order to look for hidden carvings and inscriptions, or to discover whence the man's distant forefathers had obtained their building material. Some suspecting a deposit of coal under the soil began to dig for it, and forgot even the stones. They all said "This tower is most interesting." But they also said (after pushing it over): "What a muddle it is in!" And even the man's own descendants, who might have been expected to consider what he had been about, were heard to murmur, "He is such an odd fellow. Imagine his using these old stones just to build a nonsensical tower! Why did he not restore the old house? He had no sense of proportion." **But from the top of that tower the man had been able to look out upon the sea.**

IF I CAN UNDERSTAND IT, IT CAN'T BE MUCH GOOD

Although his reputation was restored when it was discovered that his poetry had a cynical side, Robert Frost was for a long time an object of amusement. The modern sensibility sees snowy woods and stone walls as poor substitutes for urban blight and jackhammer symphonies, and it was not gentle to the New Hampshire farmer who wrote of birches. I am speaking, of course, of the artier-than-thou crowd, not the common folk who recited his poems or the Pulitzer prize committee that honored him four times. If you were a "real" poet in 1960, at least among my wannabee pals, you smirked a little when Frost read at Kennedy's inauguration. Pound was fine, and Yeats, and of course Eliot. Frost was just too easy to understand.

Besides, he rhythmed and rhymed—perhaps his greatest sin against modernity. Poetry, we Eliot apes knew in 1960, should scar, not scan, and it should not under any circumstances fall into the moon-spoon-June rut that was fit only for Ogden Nash and your kid sister's diary. For free souls, free verse.

Frost's own comment on free verse was humorously dismissive. As a working poet, he realized, as of course Eliot realized, that formal restraints were intended to challenge, not block, the imagination. Write "free" verse? He told a *Newsweek* interviewer, **"I'd just as soon play tennis with the net down."**

GRAMMAR MADE (SL)EASY

A writer whose name escapes me was once asked by a novice what qualities it took to make it in his profession. The older man said simply, **"Do you like sentences?"** This solid, craftsmanlike response zeroed in on the nuts and bolts that writing entails.

One writer who clearly likes sentences is the humorist-grammarian Karen Elizabeth Gordon. "Humorist" and "grammarian" may sound like mutually exclusive terms, but Gordon's grammar handbook *The Transitive Vampire* (1984) proves they're not. Illustrating the rules of English grammar with sentences that are as exotic as they are appropriate, Gordon comes up with deliciously twisted examples to show:

The use of a subordinate conjunction: **"*If* Lucifer confesses, we'll let the rest of you go."**

Subject-verb agreement: **"An aficionado and a cretin *are* sharing a pitcher of beer."**

Pronominal agreement: **"The Styrian String Quartet is a four-headed monster of catgut and mediocrity that shouldn't be let out of *its* cage."**

The semicolon: **"She wrapped herself in an enigma; there was no other way to keep warm."**

Last but not least, the infinitive phrase: **"To be ultimately satisfying, a tryst should coincide with several other transgressions as well."**

Grammar and epigrammar in one package. George Bernard Shaw couldn't have done it better.

• • •

BURIED VOICES

In the past two decades, feminist criticism has become the darling of the academies. Entire rafts of hitherto unsuspected masterpieces by women have been unearthed by assiduous foremother-hunters, while the vast edifice of Western culture has been trashed, critically speaking, as little more than patriarchy's bastard. While this effort has convinced only feminist ideologues that the memoirs of a Nicaraguan peasant woman should supplant Shakespeare in the literary canon, the charge that women's writings have been neglected is impossible to deny unless you're an ideologue of the MCP persuasion. The French writer Christine de Pisan made the point as far back as the fifteenth century, in her attack on the allegedly misogynistic *Romance of the Rose:* "**It is not the women who have written the books.**" A more recent, and slyer, version of the complaint is the bumper sticker "**Anonymous was a woman.**"

chapter 9

Daffynitions

A Glossary of Glibness

Many of the quirkiest and most illuminating observations are to be found in the form of toss-off definitions (those rib-nudging, brain-tickling one-liners that *Reader's Digest* called "daffynitions"). Seldom do these small exercises in subversive lexicography carry the anecdotal freight of longer comments, although they certainly display their authors' personalities and views of life. This chapter contains a hundred or so of these often telling, often infuriating, "anti-Websterisms."

Actor. 1. "A man with an infinite capacity for taking praise" (Michael Redgrave) 2. "The only honest hypocrite" (William Hazlitt)
Adultery. "The application of democracy to love" (H. L. Mencken)
Advertising. "The rattling of a stick inside a swill bucket" (George Orwell)
Age. 1. "Fifteen years older than I am" (Bernard Baruch) 2. "Something that doesn't matter unless you're a cheese" (Billie Burke)
Architecture. "Frozen music" (Johann Wolfgang Goethe)
Aristocrat. "A democrat with his pockets full" (Josh Billings)
Art. "A lie that makes us realize the truth" (Pablo Picasso)

Atheist. 1. "A man who has no invisible means of support" (John Buchan) 2. "A guy who watches a Notre Dame–SMU football game and doesn't care who wins" (Dwight D. Eisenhower)

Baby. 1. "A bald head and a pair of lungs" (Eugene Field) 2. "God's opinion that the world should go on" (Carl Sandburg)

Bank. "A place that will lend you money if you can prove you don't need it" (Joe E. Lewis)

Budget. "A mythical beanbag. Congress votes mythical beans into it, and then tries to reach in and pull real beans out." (Will Rogers)

Bureaucracy. "An execution chamber in which the condemned are alternately strangled by rules, clubbed with paper, and starved in lines" (Alexander Yarrowville)

Cauliflower. "Cabbage with a college education" (Mark Twain)

Celebrity. 1. "A person who works hard all his life to become well known, then wears dark glasses to avoid being recognized" (Fred Allen) 2. "A person who is known for his well knownness" (Daniel Boorstin)

Chance. "The pseudonym of God when He did not want to sign" (Anatole France)

Cheese. "Milk's leap to immortality" (Clifton Fadiman)

Christianity. "One beggar telling another beggar where he found bread" (D. T. Niles)

Civilization. "The attempt to reduce force to being the last resort" (José Ortega y Gasset)

Classical Music. "The kind we keep thinking will turn into a tune" (Kin Hubbard)

Communism. 1. "A mighty, unifying thunderstorm, marking the springtime of mankind" (Nikita Khrushchev) 2. "Nobody's got nothing, but everybody's working" (Fred Allen) 3. "The opiate of the intellectuals" (Clare Boothe Luce)

Conceit. "God's gift to little men" (Bruce Barton)

Conservative. 1. "A man with two perfectly good legs who, however, has never learned to walk" (Franklin D. Roosevelt) 2. "A man who wants the rules enforced so no one can make a pile the way he did" (Gregory Nunn)

Critic. "A legless man who teaches running" (Channing Pollack)

Cynic. 1. "A man who knows the price of everything and the value of nothing" (Oscar Wilde) 2. "A man who, when he smells flowers, looks around for a coffin" (H. L. Mencken) 3. "Just a man who found out when he was ten that there wasn't any Santa Claus, and he's still upset" (James Gould Cozzens)

Death. 1. "The cure for all diseases" (Thomas Browne) 2. "A low chemical trick played on everybody but sequoia trees" (J. J. Furnas)

Deceit. "A dead wasp with a live tail" (Josh Billings)

Diplomacy. "The art of saying 'Nice doggie' until you can find a rock" (Will Rogers)

Distance. "The only thing the rich are willing for the poor to call theirs, and keep" (Ambrose Bierce)

Divorce. 1. "A hash made of domestic scraps" (Ed Wynn) 2. "Holy deadlock" (A. P. Herbert) 3. "Fission after fusion" (Rita Mae Brown)

Drama. "Life with the dull bits left out" (Alfred Hitchcock)

Drunkard. "A person who tries to pull himself out of trouble with a corkscrew" (Edward Baldwin)

Epigram. "A platitude with vine leaves in its hair" (H. L. Mencken)

Etiquette. "The noise you don't make while eating soup" (Leonard Levinson)

Expert. "Someone who knows more and more about less and less" (Nicholas Murray Butler)

Fame. "What someone writes on your tombstone" (Finley Peter Dunne)

Fanatic. 1. "A man who does what he thinks the Lord would do if He knew the facts of the case" (Finley Peter Dunne) 2. "One who can't change his mind and won't change the subject" (Winston Churchill)

Fool. 1. "One who does not suspect himself" (José Ortega y Gasset) 2. "Anybody who feels at ease in the world today" (Robert Maynard Hutchins)

France. "A long despotism tempered by epigrams" (Thomas Carlyle)

Golf. 1. "A plague invented by the Calvinistic Scots as a punishment for man's sins" (James Reston) 2. "A good walk spoiled" (Mark Twain)

Gossip. "News running ahead of itself in a red satin dress" (Liz Smith)

Gourmet. "A glutton with brains" (Phillip Haberman, Jr.)

Guilt. "The gift that keeps on giving" (Erma Bombeck)

Hatred. "The coward's revenge for being intimidated" (George Bernard Shaw)

Heathen. "A man who has never played baseball" (Elbert Hubbard)

Highbrow. 1. "A person educated beyond his intelligence" (Brander Matthews) 2. "The kind of person who looks at a sausage and thinks of Picasso" (A. P. Herbert)

Hygiene. "The corruption of medicine by morality" (H. L. Mencken)

Idealist. "One who, on noticing that a rose smells better than a cabbage, concludes that it will also make better soup" (H. L. Mencken)

Impressionism. "The newspaper of the soul" (Henri Matisse)

Intellectual. "A man who takes more words than necessary to tell us more than he knows" (Dwight D. Eisenhower)

Jazz. "Music invented by demons for. the torture of imbeciles" (Henry van Dyke)

Jury. "Twelve persons chosen to decide who has the better lawyer" (Robert Frost)

Las Vegas. "Everyman's cut-rate Babylon" (Alistair Cooke)

Liberal. 1. "A mind that is able to imagine itself believing anything" (Max Eastman) 2. "A man who wants to be accepted as a black but not mistaken for one" (John Killens)

Lie. "Truth in masquerade" (Lord Byron)

Life. 1. "The permission to know death" (Djuna Barnes) 2. "Just one damn thing after another" (Elbert Hubbard) 3. "One damn thing over and over" (Edna St. Vincent Millay)

Memoirs. "When you put down the good things you ought to have done and leave out the bad ones you did do" (Will Rogers)

Metaphysician. "A man who goes into a dark cellar at midnight without a light looking for a black cat that is not there" (Bowen of Colwood)

Missionaries. "Sincere, self-deceived persons suffering from meddler's itch" (Elbert Hubbard)

Music. "The brandy of the damned." (George Bernard Shaw)

Narcissist. "Someone better looking than you" (Gore Vidal)

New York. 1. "The nation's thyroid gland" (Christopher Morley) 2. "Skyscraper National Park" (Kurt Vonnegut) 3. "A narrow island off the coast of New Jersey devoted to the pursuit of lunch" (Raymond Sokolov)

News. 1. "The cultivation of disquietude for disquietude's sake" (Aldous Huxley) 2. "History shot on the wing" (Gene Fowler)

Novel. "A mirror walking along a main road" (Stendhal)

Opportunist. "One who goes ahead and does what you always intended to do" (K. L. Kirchbaum)

Optimist. 1. "A fellow who believes what's going to happen will be postponed" (Kin Hubbard) 2. "Someone who tells you to cheer up when things are going his way" (Edward R. Murrow)

Painting. "The art of protecting flat surfaces from the weather and exposing them to the critic" (Ambrose Bierce)

Pâté. "A French meatloaf that's had a couple of cocktails" (Carol Cutler)

Patriotism. 1. "The last refuge of a scoundrel" (Samuel Johnson) 2. "The veneration of real estate over principles" (George Jean Nathan)

Peanut Butter. "The pâté of childhood" (Florence Fabricant)

Pedant. 1. "A person who knows all the answers but doesn't understand the questions" (Warren Goldberg) 2. "A talkative footnote" (Eugene Brussell)

Pessimist. 1. "A man who thinks everybody as nasty as himself, and hates them for it" (George Bernard Shaw) 2. "One who builds dungeons in the air" (Walter Winchell)

Poetry. 1. "The deification of reality" (Edith Sitwell) 2. "The impish attempt to paint the color of the wind" (Maxwell Bodenheim) 3. "A sliver of the moon lost in the belly of a golden frog" (Carl Sandburg)

Professor. "One who talks in someone else's sleep" (W. H. Auden)

Prose. "Where all the lines but the last go on to the margin— poetry is where some of them fall short" (Jeremy Bentham)

Prude. "A coquette gone to seed" (Josh Billings)

Psychoanalysis. "Confession without absolution" (G. K. Chesterton)

Radical. "A man with both feet planted firmly in the air" (Franklin D. Roosevelt)

Realist. "A man who insists on making the same mistakes his grandfather did" (Benjamin Disraeli)

Reformer. 1. "One who is trying to make the world a better place to die in" (Leonard Levinson) 2. "A guy who rides through a sewer in a glass-bottomed boat" (Jimmie Walker)

Repartee. "What you wish you'd said" (Heywood Broun)

Rock 'n' Roll. "Monotony tinged with hysteria" (Vance Packard)

Scoundrel. "A man who won't stay bought" (William Tweed)

Sex. 1. "The central problem of life" (Havelock Ellis) 2. The great amateur art" (David Cort) 3. "The poor man's polo" (Clifford Odets)

Slang. "Language that rolls up its sleeves, spits on its hands, and goes to work" (Carl Sandburg)

Spain. "A whale stranded upon the coast of Europe" (Edmund Burke)

Sports. "The toy department of human life" (Howard Cosell)

Sweat. "The cologne of accomplishment" (Heywood Broun)

Taxpayer. "Someone who works for the federal government but who doesn't have to take a civil service examination" (Ronald Reagan)

Television. 1. "A vast wasteland" (Newton Minow) 2. "A medium of entertainment which permits millions of people to listen to the same joke at the same time and yet remain lonesome" (T. S. Eliot) 3. "Chewing gum for the eyes" (John Mason Brown)

Theory. "A hunch with a college education" (J. A. Carter)

Tyrant. "A slave turned inside out" (Herbert Spencer)

Virus. "A Latin word used by doctors to mean, 'Your guess is as good as mine'" (Bob Hope)

Weed. "A flower in the wrong place" (Edward Stokes)

Work. "The curse of the drinking classes" (Oscar Wilde)

Worry. "Interest paid on trouble before it becomes due" (William Inge)

Writer. "A schmuck with an Underwood" (Jack Warner)

chapter 10

Snappy Comebacks...

Retorts

A DOG'S LIFE

The English word *cynic* derives from the Greek philosophers of the fourth century B.C. whose fellow Athenians called them *cynikoi,* or "dogs," because of their slovenly appearance and disdain for convention. The cynics believed that the pursuit of virtue required rejecting material comfort and social amenities, and to that end they embraced an ostentatiously unpretentious life-style which, to the good citizens they encountered, was outrageous if not actually sociopathic. Like the hardcore teenage rebels of today, the cynics were seen as PWA, or "punks with an attitude."

The most outragous of this renegade crew was Diogenes of Sinope, who died in 323. To show his lack of respect for Athenian creature comforts, Diogenes lived in a washtub, owned nothing but the clothes on his back and a bowl, and even gave away the bowl, according to legend, after he saw a child drink from his hands. To demonstrate his scorn for the city's conventional notions of morality, he wandered the streets in daylight holding up a lantern, supposedly in search of "one honest man." You would not invite Diogenes in for wine and feta.

For reasons that are not explained in the historical record, Alexander the Great, who was not particularly Spartan in his own tastes, found Diogenes's orneriness attractive. The lure of opposites, maybe, or the same motive that made Andrew Carnegie give away his money. Whatever the reason, the young conqueror's admiration afforded Diogenes an opportunity for his best line. Alexander came up to him one day while he was scratching formulas in the sand with a stick. Standing over him, the master of the known world promised to grant him any wish he wanted. "Just name it." Sure, said Diogenes. **"Stand out of my light."**

THE WICKED MR. WILKES

The British parliamentarian John Wilkes (1727–1797) helped to extend the limits of free speech in England by publicly opposing the policies of George III in his journal *The North Briton*. After a particularly scurrilous attack in 1763, he was expelled from the House of Commons and tried for treason; his acquittal by the courts was a landmark step toward civil liberties.

As fine a figurehead as Wilkes may have been for free expression, his sharp tongue and love of faction made him enemies, even among those who had once been his friends. One of his friends, the Earl of Sandwich (1718–1792), helped to prosecute him in 1763, and during the proceedings fed him a classic ad hominem straight line: **"You, Sir, will die either on the gallows or of the pox."** "That, Sir," shot back Wilkes, **"must depend on whether I embrace your principles or your mistress."**

EASIER SAID THAN DONE

By all accounts but his own, Alexander Smyth was a windbag. A Virginia lawyer, soldier, and legislator, he achieved an unhappy national prominence during the War of 1812 as the commander of a brigade attempting to invade Canada. Given the ill-trained and dispirited nature of his troops, his decision to abort the mission was militarily sound, and it's likely no one would have given him much grief about it had he not preceded the attempt with boastful posturing, promising the "immediate conquest" of the British domain. But his busy mouth had painted such a rosy picture of American victory that when it failed he was universally reviled—even accused of cowardice by a junior officer. The charge led to a duel from which both parties escaped unharmed, but the injury had already been done to Smyth's reputation. Moral: If it's easier said than done, do it first.

In spite of the invasion debacle, the general retained enough popularity in his home state to be elected repeatedly to Congress for over a dozen years. In Washington, where bombast was a way of life, he earned a floor reputation as what John Bartlett called a "tedious" speaker, and his performance there elicited a bored retort from the Great Pacificator, Kentucky's Henry Clay. Clay, who had fought a duel himself over his unorthodox elevation to the vice-presidency in 1825, differed during a debate with the ex-general, and was informed by him, "**You, sir, speak for the present generation, but I speak for posterity.**" Without missing a beat, Clay responded, "**Yes, and you seem resolved to speak until the arrival of your audience.**"

THE GREAT PACIFICATOR PACIFIED

Virginia Congressman John Randolph (1773–1833) possessed one of the more cutting wits in Washington history, and he used it to merciless effect against his rivals. The best known of these was the House Speaker Henry Clay (1777–1852), with whom Randolph had a famous run-in in 1825. In that year Clay had been made secretary of state in a seeming deal that many, even in his own party, considered irregular. Clay, Andrew Jackson, and John Quincy Adams had all run for president in 1824; none had received a majority of the votes; and Clay had gotten the secretary's job as an apparent trade-off for throwing his votes to Adams. "**Corrupt bargain**" was the cry raised by the disappointed Jacksonians, and nobody raised it longer or louder than John Randolph.

That wasn't all he said. In Randolph's mind, Clay even before the bargain was like a "**rotten mackeral by moonlight**"—undeniably brilliant in his political dealing, but just as undeniably stinking. He needled Clay constantly about the backroom deal and, according to a popular Washington story, also bested him in a famous exchange of wits that recalled the bridge meeting of Friar Tuck and Robin Hood. On a narrow walk in the nation's capital, the two approached each other until it was clear one would have to give way. Clay announced proudly, "**I, Sir, never step aside for a scoundrel.**" Randolph immediately stepped into the gutter and responded, "**On the other hand, I always do.**"

The bad blood between the two men came to a head in a duel in 1826. The outcome was uneventful, with both men retiring from the field with their honors and torsos intact. But the "corrupt bargain" charge never really disappeared; it was a stain on Clay's reputation for the rest of his life. Randolph, who was a master at holding grudges, didn't forget it even in death. At his request he was buried facing West, so he could keep an eye on his rival from Kentucky.

STONE WALLS DO NOT A PRISON MAKE

Most of us remember Henry David Thoreau for two acts of social and personal defiance. Each one created a memorable piece of writing, and each one is often attended by misunderstanding. The first act is his two-year sojourn at Walden Pond, which gave us *Walden* and the image of the Concord recluse. The misunderstanding here lies in the fact that, on almost every day on those two years, the "recluse" either welcomed visitors from nearby Concord or walked to the village himself for food and chitchat. His famous experiment in getting away from society, therefore, was also a romantic exercise in hedging his bets.

Much the same thing can be said about his second act of tweaking conventions: his incarceration for refusing to pay a war tax. "Civil Disobedience" explains why he went to jail to protest the Mexican War, but it's a little vague on the particulars of his internment. Modern war resisters look to Thoreau as a moral model, and Gandhi himself was politically influenced by the famous essay. What they usually forget is that Thoreau languished behind bars just one night before a benefactor (some say Emerson, others say Thoreau's aunt) paid the tax for him and bailed him out. That doesn't diminish the philosophical value of

"Civil Disobedience," but it does suggest a reassessment of Henry's "sacrifice."

To be fair to him, it should be pointed out that he yelled long and hard about the bailout, and that his brief stay did elicit one great (although possibly apocryphal) line. Going to see his friend in stir, Emerson asked ingenuously, **"What are you doing in there?"** According to legend, Henry responded, **"What are you doing *out?*"**

HAWK AND DOVE

Among Benjamin Disraeli's many political enemies was the Manchester Liberal John Bright (1811–1889), who like William Gladstone was a reformer at home and a dove abroad. Bright came to prominence in the 1840s by standing with Gladstone against the Corn Laws. Throughout the century, he questioned his nation's foreign adventures, speaking against the Crimean War and intervention in China in the 1850s and, decades later, resigning from the government altogether to protest the British bombardment of Egypt. This was entirely in character for a man who had been raised a Quaker, but it didn't sit very well with Dizzy's concept of empire. When one of Bright's admirers pointed out that he was a self-made man, Disraeli responded, **"I know he is, and he adores his maker."**

OUTFOPPED AGAIN

To admirers of conversation, it's hard to imagine anyone wittier than Oscar Wilde. He goes down in everyone's Pundit Pantheon, along with George Bernard Shaw, as one of Ireland's inestimable gifts to the history of chitchat. In the Yellow Decade, however, Wilde had his rivals, among them the American painter James McNeill Whistler.

Known today as the perpetrator of *Whistler's Mother* (actually entitled *Arrangement in Grey and Black, No. 1*), Whistler was considered in his own day a daring innovator, and was as much in demand as Wilde himself for dinner parties. He was also, like Wilde, a dandified "aesthete," meaning that he believed artists were, or at least should be, governed by different rules than "duller" folk. He contributed strongly to Wilde's appreciation of this elitist doctrine, and he made sure that the younger man didn't forget it.

On one occasion, speaking to art critic Humphrey Ward in Wilde's presence, Whistler cautioned him never to use the terms "good" and "bad." Instead, he advised, "Say 'I like this and I dislike that' and you'll be within your right. And now, come and have a whiskey. You're sure to like that." Impressed by the cleverness of the segue, Wilde told the painter, **"I wish I had said that."** Whistler replied, **"You will, Oscar, you will."**

OR, FOR THAT MATTER, LEONARDO

Whistler was no less haughty with his fans than he was with fellow professionals like Ruskin and Wilde. He had about as high a regard for his own talents as any painter who ever lived, and those who failed to recognize his "self-evident" preeminence sometimes found themselves on the end of a barb. One well-meaning admirer thought to compliment him by comparing him with the great Spanish painter Diego Velázquez. **"I only know of two painters in the world,"** she gushed, **"yourself and Velázquez."** Whistler responded, **"Why drag in Velázquez?"**

WSC VS. GBS

According to William Manchester's mammoth biography of Winston Churchill, *The Last Lion,* Churchill knew George Bernard Shaw well and was even influenced in his concern for the poor by talks with Shaw and his Fabian friends, Beatrice and Sidney Webb. Shaw for his part respected the blustery lion, partly out of fellow feeling and partly, perhaps, because he saw in him a model case of dogged resilience. When the British turned to Churchill in their darkest hour after years of scoffing at his warnings about Hitler, Shaw remembered, **"The moment we got a good fright, and had to find a man who could and would do something, we were on our knees to Winston Churchill."**

As might be expected of two such outsized characters, their exchanges could produce sparks as well as plaudits. One flurry flew, humorously, in 1913. Rehearsals for Shaw's comedy *Pygmalion* had just ended in London, and the playwright sent Churchill a needling invitation: **"Am reserving two tickets for you for my premier. Come and bring a friend—if you have one."** Unflustered, Churchill wired back: **"Impossible to be present for the first performance. Will attend the second—if there is one."**

FROM SOUP TO NUTS

Nancy Astor, born Nancy Langhorne and generally known as Lady Astor, was the first woman to sit as a member of the British Parliament and, for decades, one of the realm's most colorful polemicists. Born in Virginia in 1879, she married the British heir to the Waldorf-Astoria fortune in 1906, inherited his seat in the Commons when he went on to the Lords, and stayed there, quipping and sniping, until 1945. When she died in 1964, she had attained in British social life the same kind of eccentric grande dame quality as that shown by Alice Roosevelt Longworth on the American side. Like Mrs. Longworth a political conservative, Lady Astor also staunchly defended women's rights, tried to introduce Prohibition into England, and was identified unhappily in the 1930s with the "Clivedon set," favoring appeasement of Hitler's Germany.

On at least the latter two counts, she might have been expected to rub Winston Churchill the wrong way, and the two MPs did have their ups and downs. **"My vigor, vitality, and cheek repel me. I am the kind of woman I would run from,"** she said of herself in the 1950s. Churchill in one famous exchange endorsed that assessment. The occasion was a dinner party at which some clever hostess, no doubt hoping for sparks to fly, sat Churchill and Lady Astor near each other. She was not disappointed. At one point Lady Astor said distinctly, **"Winston, if I were your wife, I'd poison your soup."** Churchill replied, **"Nancy, if I were your husband, I'd drink it."**

. . .

THE CRIER CONNED

Franklin P. Adams (1881–1960), known to his many readers as
FPA, wrote a popular New York newspaper column "The Conning
Tower" from 1913 to 1941, and in the war years delighted millions
with his "Information Please" radio show—a kind of pre-*Jeopardy* trivia
show, without the prizes. His pal and rival Alexander Woollcott (1887–
1943) also contributed to the New York press (theater reviews laced
with lots of gossip), and had *his* own radio show, "The Town Crier,"
which ran successfully for over a dozen years.

Since the two were also charter members of the Algonquin Hotel's
famed Round Table, it might be expected that a flash of repartee might
occasionally link them. One such flash—worthy of the Whistler-Wilde
rivalry—was recorded in 1922. Woollcott had just gathered a collection
of his essays into a volume entitled *Shouts and Whispers*. At a signing
party, with pen in hand, he cooed to Adams, **"Ah, what is so rare
as a Woollcott first edition?"** FPA's reply: **"A Woollcott second
edition."**

IVORY TICKLERS

When they met around 1930, George Gershwin (1898–1937) was
the established king of American popular classical music; Oscar Levant
(1906–1972) was an aspiring concert pianist earning his living writing
scores for Hollywood films. Levant soon put his own compositional
dreams to the side to become Gershwin's devoted admirer and public
interpreter. The two had more than professional respect going for their
friendship, however, as was evident in a warmly bantering exchange.
Reflecting on the gloomy-Gus narcissism that Levant developed into a
public persona, Gershwin once asked him, **"If you had it all over
again, would you fall in love with yourself?"** Levant replied with
a mocking request: **"Why don't you play us a medley of your
hit?"**

Most good repartee works because it's accurate as well as sharp.
This one works in spite of its blatant inaccuracy. By the time Gershwin

succumbed to a brain tumor at the age of thirty-eight, his hits included the American classics "Swanee" (popularized by Al Jolson), *Rhapsody in Blue, An American in Paris,* and *Porgy and Bess.* Of these, only *Porgy* was composed after he met Levant.

UPPERCUTS FROM DOWN UNDER

The reigning giant of Australia's postwar recovery, the Liberal politician Sir Robert Menzies (1894–1978) fought for free enterprise and social justice at home and closer ties to the United States in international affairs. An extremely popular leader, he first served in Parliament in the 1930s, became prime minister briefly at the outbreak of World War II, and held the post again for almost twenty years after the war. Not until the 1970s was the hegemony of his Liberal party seriously challenged.

Not everyone loved him, of course. As a parliamentarian he was perceived by fellow legislators to be somewhat aloof, which led one detractor to accuse him of having a superiority complex. His response to the charge showed a flair for repartee: **"Considering the company I keep here, that is hardly surprising."** The same flair came out when a woman heckled him during an electron campaign. **"I wouldn't vote for you,"** she snapped, **"if you were the Archangel Gabriel."** Menzies replied, **"If I were the Archangel Gabriel, madam, you would not be in my constituency."**

TYPECAST—AND LOVING EVERY MINUTE

The British-born actor Archibald Leach first charmed film audiences in the 1930s when he became debonair, engagingly befuddled Cary Grant. Three decades later, he was still cracking wise, buckling female knees, and going strong. In 1970, when he received a special Academy Award for his lifetime contribution to the movies, he had been retired for less than five years and had established a legacy of light masterpieces second to none. From his early days playing opposite Mae West (**"Come up and see me sometime,"** she told him in 1933's

She Done Him Wrong), through his incomparable screwball comedy period, to his classy, laid-back work for Alfred Hitchcock, to the wonderful character role in his penultimate film, *Father Goose* (1964), Grant was the epitome of slightly rattled but effortless charm. To the fussy, he had a limited range; but as he savvily pointed out, "**I play myself to perfection.**"

His long tenure invited queries about his age, and one of them elicited a response from the actor that could have come straight out of *His Girl Friday* or *The Philadelphia Story*. A fan telegrammed Grant's agent, "**How old Cary Grant?**" On Grant's instructions, he received the following reply: "**Old Cary Grant fine. How you?**"

THE WORKMAN WORTHY OF HIS HIRE

When you console someone whose work is going slowly with the adage "**Rome wasn't built in a day,**" you're citing a proverb that was first put down on paper in 1562. The locus classicus for this saying, as for scores of other traditional words of wisdom, was the English poet John Heywood's collection of that year—a compendium that gave us, to name just a few, "A rolling stone gathers no moss," "Beggers should not be choosers," "A penny for your thoughts," "I know which side my bread is buttered on," and "That hits the nail on the head."

When Lyndon Johnson was majority leader of the Senate, two of his fellow senators paid grudging homage to his reputation as a taskmaster in a humorous update of the "Rome" line. Johnson had kept the upper house in late session, as was his wont when there was business still unattended to. "What's the hurry?" one of the senators asked the other. "Rome wasn't built in a day." "**That's right,**" responded the other. "**But Lyndon Johnson wasn't foreman on that job.**"

Somehow this always reminds me of Sam the tailor, who is confronted by an impatient customer awaiting a suit. "You've been working on it for three weeks now, Sam. It only took God six days to make the entire *world*." "**That's right,**" acknowledges Sam. "**And look at it.**"

FLOAT LIKE A BUTTERFLY, FALL LIKE A STONE

Public modesty was not Muhammad Ali's strong suit. Some say he played the boastful clown for psychological effect, intimidating his opponents with humorous puffing even before they got into the ring. Others say that when he called himself "The Greatest," he meant it. However serious he was about the persona, it provided years of entertainment for his fans—and once gave him a kick as well, when it was turned against him. He was on a plane that was about to take off and had forgotten to fasten his safety belt. When a flight attendant reminded him to buckle up, he laughed, "**Superman don't need no seat belt.**" The attendant laughed back, "**Superman don't need no airplane.**"

THOSE WILD AND CRAZY POST-SOCRATICS

The American philosopher Raymond Smullyan first came to my attention ten years ago with an infuriatingly funny book of paradoxes called, paradoxically enough, *What Is the Name of This Book?* In a subsequent collection of brain ticklers entitled *5000 B.C. and Other Philosophical Fantasies,* he cites a conversation with the logical positivist O. Bowsma which shows that even folks who spend 98 percent of their lives contemplating the eternal verities can find time for an occasional old-fashioned put-down.

Discussing the ancient question of whether or not matter exists independent of our cognition, Smullyan takes what he calls an "extreme" view, suggesting that minds are independent of bodies. This being the case, he assures Bowsma, he can readily imagine himself occupying another physical form. "I am fully prepared for the possibility that next week I might find myself in a totally different body, say, one with three arms." Bowsma asks him slyly, "**Have you bought yourself another glove?**"

As the conversation proceeds, Smullyan becomes more and more "idealistic" (he means idealistic like Bishop Berkeley, not like a re-former) until an exasperated Bowsma, attempting to keep physical reality in mind, is raising objections to every statement that he makes. "Tell me," Smullyan asks finally, "do you believe I am being inconsistent?" "No," Bowsma replies. Whereupon "another philosopher present," who sadly remains unidentified, undercuts them both with the observation, **"What you are saying is too *vague* to be inconsistent."**

chapter 11

...And
Other Cuts

Insults

THE SCOURGE OF PRINCES

Six months before Columbus first sighted land in the Caribbean, a shoemaker's wife in Arezzo gave birth to a son who would terrify princes. Pietro Aretino moved to Rome as a young man, where he ingratiated himself to the courtly set by passing himself off as a noble, then quickly fell out of favor by writing lampoons about the high life and lewd sonnets. Leaving Rome for Venice, he continued to publish attacks on Roman excess while making friends with the painter Titian (who did his portrait), writing comedies about life among the workers, and gaining the kind of slavish-nervous following that in this century surrounded H. L. Mencken. His biographer Thomas Chubb called him **"the first blackmailer, the first journalist, and the first publicity man."** His contemporary Ludovico Ariosto, reflecting the ambivalence that his poison pen elicited, called him **"divine Aretino"** and **"the scourge of princes."**

Since he had had little praise to dispense during his lifetime, his enemies responded with none upon his death. It came to him in the form of a stroke in 1556, as he was leaning back in a chair, laughing, in a tavern. One former victim of his satire took advantage of the tableau to spread the tale that he had been laughing about his own sisters' sexual escapades. Others made up last words for him, including a vulgar reference to the oil of Extreme Unction: "**Keep me from the rats, now that I'm greasy.**" And both his friends and his enemies created epitaphs.

One friendly epitaph, which graces his tomb, thanked him for "ridiculing the vices of the world." An unfriendly one, much funnier, went as follows:

> *Qui giace Aretino, poeta tosco,*
> *Chi disse mal d'ognan fuorche Dio,*
> *Scusandosi col dir, Non lo conosco.*

The English runs:

> **Here lies Aretino, the Tuscan poet.**
> **He spoke ill of everybody but God**
> **And excused himself by saying, I didn't know Him.**

THE MOUTH THAT ROARED

Thomas Babington Macaulay (1800–1859) combined a distinguished though brief career in Parliament with a passion for literature and "literary" language that made his writing a model for English stylists. In Parliament, his stunning oratory helped win passage for the Reform Bill of 1832—the first step in Britain's move toward universal suffrage. As a government official in India, he pushed for English-language education and almost by himself drafted the colony's penal code. The essays he wrote for the *Edinburgh Review* brought his finely crafted criticism to a wide audience, and the history of England that he worked on for almost twenty years remained a standard font of patriotic pride into this century. At his death he had earned his nation's highest literary honor: burial in Westminster Abbey.

His marvelous prose, however, evidently worked better in print than in person. It was all well and good to hold forth interminably on the floor of Parliament, but that sort of thing gets irritating quickly in private company, and Macaulay's conversation overwhelmed, rather than won over, some of his listeners. Florence Nightingale called it **"a procession of one."** Sydney Smith, an irrepressibly witty clergyman who helped to found the *Edinburgh Review,* said of its famous contributor, **"He has occasional flashes of silence that make his conversation perfectly delightful."**

An even better dig came from William Lamb (Lord Melbourne), a Whig politician whose opposition to reform was so consistent that his standard response to a call for change was the rhetorical query **"Why not leave it alone?"** Both politically and personally, he found the voluble Macaulay hard to take. **"I wish I was as cocksure of anything,"** he once sighed, **"as Tom Macaulay is of everything."**

DUELING GIANTS

William Ewart Gladstone (1809–1898), English liberalism's "Grand Old Man" of the Victorian era, fought for religious toleration, Irish home rule, and the application of Anglican high-mindedness to international involvements. His colorful Conservative rival, Benjamin Disraeli (1804–1881), although a leader of his party's reform wing, stood against him on most critical issues, supporting electoral "moderation" at home and imperialism abroad. They were not bosom chums. They clashed first in the 1840s, when Gladstone wanted to abolish, and Disraeli wanted to sustain, the protectionist Corn Laws that kept market prices up for wealthy farmers. Thirty years later they were still at it, with Gladstone publicly denouncing Disraeli for his supposed indifference to Turkish atrocities in the Balkans.

Disraeli, who had begun his career as a novelist, had a sharper tongue and quicker wit than the Grand Old Man, and their rivalry is best enshrined in one of his jabs. When asked to define the difference between a misfortune and a calamity, Disraeli suggested, **"If Gladstone fell into the Thames, that would be a misfortune, and if anybody pulled him out, that . . . would be a calamity."**

NOTICING THE CRACK IN THE LIBERTY BELL

Most Americans, for most of the nation's history, have labored under the delusion that they are different. Fatuities like "God's country," "the chosen people," and "the greatest country on earth" have informed our sense of ourselves since the Declaration. It's sobering, therefore, to encounter the other side—epigrammatic hints from both within and without that the planet's first popular democracy has its faults.

Of such hints, British sage Samuel Johnson's is the most economically caustic. Shortly after the American Revolution, he vowed, **"I am willing to love all mankind, except an American."** French statesman George Clemenceau was more expansive. He called America **"the only nation in history that has gone from barbarism to decadence without passing through the intervening stage of civilization."** Our own Oliver Wendell Holmes, in his chatty *Autocrat of the Breakfast Table,* acknowledged that other lands might hold allurements that ours did not when he remarked, **"Good Americans, when they die, go to Paris."** The funniest swipe, in my opinion, was Porfirio Díaz's. Díaz was the last despotic ruler of our southern neighbor, before the 1910 revolution kicked him out. Giving an early expression to Latin American anti-Yanqui-ism, he sighed dramatically, **"Poor Mexico! So far from God and so close to the United States."**

THE BARON AND THE COWBOY

When Theodore Roosevelt succeeded the assassinated William McKinley as president in 1901, the robber barons looked over their shoulders and grabbed their checkbooks. Nobody knew for sure what TR's attitudes toward the giant monopolies, or "trusts," would be, but the consensus was that it would be less accommodating than that of McKinley, who had been an agreeable rubber stamp for business interests. Most businessmen shared the dismay of Republican kingmaker Mark Hanna, who moaned upon Roosevelt's elevation, **"Now look. That goddamned cowboy is president of the United States."**

Teddy proved to be less antitrust than his "trust-busting" reputation would suggest, but he did pounce on business for its more egregious abuses and in the process got the regulatory ball rolling. His first big attack came in 1902 on the Northern Securities Company controlled by J. P. Morgan. When the holding company was cited for restraint of trade, Morgan's first reaction was the time-honored checkbook ploy. **"If we have done anything wrong,"** he told TR, **"send your man to my man and they can fix it up."** No dice, said TR. The lawyers moved forward, eventually dissolving one of the largest "combinations" in America.

Morgan didn't exactly fold up his tent and retire after this defeat. When he died in 1913, he was still one of the great moguls of the Gilded Age, and his bequests to the doyens of culture in New York City helped to establish the Metropolitan Museum of Art and the Morgan Library. Four years before his death, as recently retired Roosevelt was preparing to go on African safari, the finance king took his revenge in an acerbic toast. According to Joseph Gardner's biography of TR as ex-president, *Departed Glory,* when Morgan heard about his old foe's plans for big game hunting, he snapped out gleefully, **"Health to the lions!"**

STEEL FLANKED BY MUSH

Teddy Roosevelt inherited the highest office in the land from a man whose unofficial administration slogan was "Stand pat," ran it for seven years at a fever pitch, and gave it up to a man who looked as if getting out of a chair would take a day's worth of effort in itself. It's unlikely that anybody this side of an adrenal gland could have matched TR for public presence and sheer energy. Certainly William McKinley and William Howard Taft were not contenders.

TR knew it, too, and swiped them both with telling lines. McKinley had taken TR on as vice-president, against the advice of his mentor Marcus Hanna, as a way of kicking him upstairs and out of New York politics. It wasn't a ticket made in heaven. After the shock of McKinley's assassination had died down, Roosevelt quipped that he had been sold to the American people like a "patent medicine." Referring to his former boss's willingness to be led—what many saw as McKinley's lack of political convictions—TR sneered that he had had "**as much backbone as a chocolate eclair.**"

To Taft, Roosevelt was somewhat more polite. The big man had been his secretary of war, after all, and his administration did carry on the reforms that Roosevelt had started. Not perfectly, of course. Taft brought twice as many antitrust suits as "trust buster" Roosevelt, but he also okayed a tariff reform that TR had resisted. He went on record as being in support of conservation, but he fired Gifford Pinchot, Roosevelt's fire-eating chief of the Forest Service. And he was too accommodating, in Roosevelt's view, to Congress's old boy network. Add it up, and this was TR's judgment: "**Taft meant well, but he meant well feebly.**"

CLUB CLUBBING

Rotary International, founded in 1905 by a Chicago lawyer, has close to one million members in over 150 countries. It got its name from the original custom of rotating meetings among members' offices, and its stated purposes include the furtherance of commercial "fellowship" and the funding of community projects and college scholarships. To anyone who isn't a member, however, it's easy to miss these noble intentions and lump Rotarians in with more foolishly fraternal and less eleemosynary organizations like, say, Ralph Cramden's Royal Order of Raccoons.

I'm not saying this is fair—only that it's a common misperception. And an old one, too. Back in the 1920s, when the Rotary had just started spinning its wheel, H. L. Mencken spotted its members as Babbit-like glad-handers: "**The first Rotarian,**" he sniffed, "**was the first man to call John the Baptist 'Jack'.**" This is equal in cleverness to my father's reading of the acronym BPOE. Members say it stands for "Benevolent and Protective Order of Elks." My father says it's code for "**Best People on Earth.**"

A VERY CLOSED CIRCLE

John Collins Bossidy, born in Massachusetts in 1860, was an eye doctor who, after several years in government service, settled down to

practice in Boston. Perhaps because he went to Holy Cross and George-
town rather than Harvard, perhaps because of the Beacon Hill crowd's
inveterate snootiness, he developed a fond distaste for Boston Brahmin
pretensions and skewered them in a famous lampoon. The occasion was
a 1910 Holy Cross alumni dinner. Bossidy offered this toast:

> **And this is good old Boston,**
> **The home of the bean and the cod,**
> **Where the Lowells talk to the Cabots**
> **And the Cabots talk only to God.**

Bossidy picked on the Cabots and Lowells not only because they
were old money but also because they were linked by intermarriage.
The Lowells were perhaps the less snooty (and less wealthy) of the two.
The family patriarch, Francis Cabot Lowell, built the country's first
modern textile mill, the Boston Manufacturing Company, in 1813; mill
town Lowell, Massachusetts, was named for him. Among those who
maintained the eminence of the Lowell name after the old man's death
were a trio of literary types: the versatile belletrist James Russell Lowell
and the poets Amy and Robert.

The Cabots' money was older and more tainted. *Their* patriarch,
the Jersey-born John Cabot (not to be confused with the explorer),
came to Salem around 1700, prospering in shipping, slave running, and
privateering. Built on this morally dubious base, the family's fortune
grew as rapidly as its reputation for snobbishness. Well before Bossidy
took out his poison pen, it was a Boston joke that the shipping clan
was **"a Massachusetts tribe known to have many customs but
no manners."** Among their descendants were two prominent U.S.
senators, Henry Cabot Lodge and his grandson, Henry Jr.

THE GREAT STONE FACE

Herbert Hoover started his public life as an engineer, and many
felt the very quality that brought him success in that profession—a
cautious, precise attention to technical details—ill suited him to lead
the country out of the Depression. His ability to tackle clearly defined,

discrete problems served him well as European relief administrator after the Great War—his efforts saved literally millions from starvation—but it was powerless against something as monstrous and diffuse as the international economic collapse of the 1930s. When he failed as president, therefore, his critics denounced him for the very skills that had earlier brought him success; like the engineeer of the "Massachusetts Miracle," Michael Dukakis, he was scorned as a man without passion, a humorless, by-the-numbers technogeek.

On a personal level this characterization seems to have fit. "Stuffed shirt" was an epithet commonly applied to Hoover while he was in the White House, and even a popular saying that purported to exculpate him of that charge admitted, **"He can give the most convincing *impersonation* of a stuffed shirt you ever saw."** Hoover's own secretary of state, Henry Stimson, acknowledged his boss's fascination with dry facts and figures by saying that a private meeting with the president was **"like sitting in a bath of ink."** The most biting comment, though, came from Gutzon Borglum, the sculptor who began work on his most famous creation, the Mount Rushmore Memorial, one year before Hoover entered office. You might have expected an artist who used dynamite as one of his tools to be more sympathetic than most of his colleagues to Hoover's stuffy "efficiency." He wasn't. His summation of the president was witheringly poetic: **"If you put a rose in Hoover's hand, it would melt."**

THE MOST HATED MAN IN AMERICA

It is a characteristic of presidents acknowledged as "great" that they are also among the most vilified persons of their time. It was true of Washington, of Jackson, and of Lincoln. It was true in spades of this century's most dynamic leader, Franklin Delano Roosevelt of Hyde Park. For every "down at the heels" working man who felt FDR's New Deal spelled economic salvation, there was a Republican party hack, a self-made millionaire, or a small businessman who felt it spelled the end of free enterprise and freedom itself. Economic conservatives branded his meddling as creeping socialism, calling him "Rooseveltski" and "Franklin Deficit Roosevelt." Isolationists claimed he was wheedling us into war.

Even some of his supporters didn't know quite what to make of someone who, born with a silver spoon in his mouth, was engineering the greatest transfer-payment scheme in U.S. history.

Public criticism of the Hyde Park dynamo ranged from the elegant to the obscene. On the polite side there was columnist Heywood Broun, echoing Henry Clay's famous pronouncement that he would rather be right than be president by observing, "**I'd rather be right than be Roosevelt.**" Toward the center of the nastiness spectrum was Washington hostess Alice Roosevelt Longworth's description of her distant cousin as "**two-thirds mush and one-third Eleanor.**" On the most biting end of the scale, few commentators outdid journalist Murray Kempton, who wrote of the president: "**I have always found Roosevelt an amusing fellow, but I would not employ him, except for reasons of personal friendship, as a geek in a common carnival.**"

PLAIN SPEAKING

Nobody remembers much about Paul Hume except that he wrote music criticism for the *Washington Post* in the 1940s and in that capacity once crossed swords with Harry Truman. The president's daughter, Margaret, was a concert singer, and it fell to Hume to review one of her performances. While admitting that she had a "pleasant" voice, he found little else to praise, suggesting with mushy sarcasm that there were "few moments during her recital when one can relax and feel confident that she will make her goal, which is the end of the song."

Harry didn't take it well. The letter that he fired off to Hume has got to be in anybody's Top Ten Insults pile, whether you measure by quotability or merely venom:

> **I have just read your lousy review buried in the back pages. You sound like a frustrated old man who never made a success, an eight-hour man on a four-ulcer job and all four ulcers working.**
>
> **I never met you, but if I do you'll need a new nose**

and a supporter below. [Conservative columnist] **Westbrook Pegler, a guttersnipe, is a gentleman compared to you. You can take that as more of an insult than a reflection on your ancestry.**

Hume printed this gem in his column, evidently believing that Harry's coarseness would do him in. It didn't. Of the thousands of letters that flowed into the White House commenting on the public tiff, four out of five sided with the president, vindicating his view, which he expressed later, that he had a perfect right to be two persons—the president of the United States and Harry Truman. "It was Harry S. Truman the human being," he said, "who wrote that note."

NOBLESSE OBLIGE—OR IS THAT MANQUÉ?

Although born to comfort and educated at Oxford, Clement Attlee (1883–1967) realized during a 1905 visit to the London slums that his calling was to work for the poor. To that end he abandoned his legal practice, entered Parliament to represent an impoverished East End constituency, and headed the Labor Party for almost twenty years. As prime minister for the second half of the 1940s, he oversaw his nation's economic recovery while implementing the nationalization of key industries, which started England on the road to welfare socialism.

You would not expect a man of such sensibilities to be enthusiastic about aristocratic traditions. Safe guess. Attlee had enough vanity to accept a spot in the peerage himself in 1955, when he was made the first Earl Attlee and Viscount Prestwood. But he was not so silly as to imagine that it meant anything. The peerage, he was well aware, was a quaint anachronism, and the House of Lords, its exclusive club, was little better. Since at least 1911, when they lost their veto power, the Lords had functioned as basically a costumed debating club, and Attlee's description of them was witheringly dismissive. **"The House of Lords,"** he once said, **"is like a glass of champagne that has stood for five days."**

THE MAN WE LOVED TO HATE

I cannot think of another American politician—or any politician, for that matter—who has been more cheerfully and widely reviled than Richard Nixon. You could fill a book with the nasty comments made about him, and do it without even dipping into the unprintable. From the time he oozed his way into the U.S. Congress by insinuating that his opponent was a Kremlin lackey to the day he paddled gloweringly out of Washington in the wake of Watergate, Nixon was the Vincent Price of the American political scene: a theatrically outré villain that you loved to hate.

Of the many barbs that Tricky Dick endured, I offer merely a handful for sad reflection. JFK, who beat him in 1960, said with patrician hauteur "**He has no taste.**" Historian Arthur Schlesinger, author of *The Paranoid Style in American History,* emphasized Nixon's doleful lack of confidence in either himself or in others: "**One has the uneasy feeling that he is always on the verge of pronouncing himself the victim of some clandestine plot.**" Harry Truman, who minced fewer words than these two Harvard boys, called him "**a shifty-eyed goddamn liar . . . one of the few in the history of this country to run for high office talking out of both sides of his mouth at the same time and lying out of both sides.**" Adlai Stevenson, who lost to the Eisenhower/Nixon ticket in 1952, stressed the same apparent duplicity that angered Truman. His summation, while less vicious than the others, is still my favorite: Nixon, he said, was "**the kind of politician who would cut down a redwood tree, then mount the stump and make a speech for conservation.**"

AFTER MANY A SUMMER DIES THE ROOSTER

Most critics of Gallic pomposity come from outside the sacred circle of *la France héroïque.* A notable exception was the poet, dramatist, filmmaker, and general cultural phenomenon Jean Cocteau (1889–1963). The embodiment of the avant-garde for almost fifty years, Cocteau helped to promote the works of Stravinsky, Picasso, and Erik Satie. He also collaborated with all of them on theater works. For the stage he not only adapted the ancient stories of Orpheus and Oedipus Rex, but also produced original texts with such modern titles as *La machine à ecrire* (The Typewriter) and *L'aigle à deux têtes* (The Two-Headed Eagle). On film he produced the surrealist classics *Le sang d'un poète* (Blood of a Poet) and *Les enfants terribles* (usually translated, a little too cutely, as The Holy Terrors). All of this work announces his resistance to "bourgeois" vision, including the delusion, so dear to the French, of national pride.

As to the latter, Cocteau once described his beloved homeland as *un coq sur un fumier,* or a rooster on a dunghill. The *coq* is of course France's national emblem, the dung what the poet thought of its patriotic bombast. This image generated a quote that is just as applicable to German, or for that matter New Guinean, nationalism as to the French. Imagining that the national symbol feeds off, rather than just resting on, the pile of platitudes, Cocteau observed, *"Otez le fumier, le coq meurt."* Roughly translated: **"Remove the shit and the rooster dies."**

A SHEEP IN WOLF'S CLOTHING

Among the British Labour party leader Denis Healey's accomplishments was his service as chancellor of the exchequer from 1974 to 1979. During that period, in good Labour fashion, he proposed budget reforms that outraged the opposition and brought charges of "fiscal irresponsibility" from Tory leaders. After one of them, Geoffrey Howe, attacked him in Parliament in 1978, Healey was asked by a reporter how he liked the heat. Devastated he wasn't. Being denounced by Howe, he said, was like **"being savaged by a dead sheep."**

THE IRON LADY AND THE PASSIONFLOWER

In the West's move to the right in the 1980s, Great Britain beat the United States by a year, when it made grocer's daughter Margaret Hilda Thatcher the first female prime minister in the nation's history.

Thatcher, who had presented herself without apology as the "Iron Lady," immediately called for the destruction of welfare socialism, a hold on inflationary labor contracts, and a return to the halcyon days of private initiative. She made it clear that dear old England would be better served if the "real" English had less competition from Commonwealth wogs— hence a crackdown on immigration became part of her plan. Like her American counterpart Mr. Reagan, she also cast a baleful eye on Communist influence, vowing to go to the wall, if need be, to keep it at bay.

Naturally, socialist England bridled under her sway, and at least two labor leaders came up with personal characterizations that deserve a place of honor in the history of insult. The first, from Marxist union leader Arthur Seargill, was an epithet. Referring to Thatcher's supposedly trigger-happy foreign policy, he called her "**the plutonium blonde.**" The second, from longtime Labour M.P. Denis Healey, was more sophisticated. He told the *New Yorker* in 1986, "**Margaret Thatcher is La Pasionaria of middle-class privilege.**" The reference was to Dolores Ibarruri, the stirring orator of the Spanish Civil War whose famous line "**No pasaran**" ("They shall not pass") became the doomed Republican forces' battle cry.

Ibarruri was also credited, incidentally, with the slogan "**It is better to die on your feet than to live on your knees.**" Many of her Communist comrades did just that, and she might have joined them after Franco's 1939 victory had she not been whisked away to the Soviet Union. She did not see Spain again until 1977, a year and a half after the Generalissimo's death.

A LITTLE BUSH-LEAGUE HUMOR

When George Bush ran for president in 1988, he did so in the face of two big obstacles. One was his social background—old money, Yale, and all that. The other was his unfortunate propensity for verbal gaffes. His announcement during the 1984 campaign about "kicking some ass" during a debate with Geraldine Ferraro; his characterization of charges that he had no overall plan for the country as "the vision thing"; his admission at one point that his strategy might be in "deep doo-doo"—these were felicities thought unbecoming of presidential candidate. You had to *get* the job before shooting yourself in the foot.

At the Democratic nominating convention that year, the keynote speaker was Texas politico Ann Richards. She fused Bush's two glaring deficits into a characterization that had more snap than the convention itself. When George makes those blunders, she told a gleeful crowd, **"He can't help himself. He was born with a silver foot in his mouth."** The delegates loved it, of course, but it did Richards a lot more good than it did them. She went on to become her state's governor. The convention's nominee, Michael Dukakis, became instant history.

RU FROM PU?

As a former Rutgers student, I am obliged to include in this chapter at least one quotation trashing Princeton. If you have not done time in New Jersey, you will perhaps know the Rutgers-Princeton rivalry as merely an athletic affair, deriving from Rutgers's 1869 victory over Princeton in the first ever college football game. It is more than that. Rutgers, the state university of New Jersey, is a public institution while Princeton is private. Rutgers is Greasy Tony subs and dollar beers at the Scarlet Knight while Princeton is chenin blanc and pâté. Rutgers is working nights and summers so your parents don't have to take a second mortgage while Princeton is worrying whether your BMW will be repainted in time for this weekend's jaunt to the Cape.

I could go on with this absolutely unbiased comparison, but let me get to the quote. It comes from Albert Einstein, who worked in Princeton from 1933 until his death. In later life he mellowed on the place, calling his stay there a kind of **"banishment to paradise."** But it's his first impression that most impresses me. It went like this, in a letter to the Queen of Belgium that he mailed from paradise a month after his arrival:

> **Princeton is a wonderful little spot, a quaint and cere-monious village of puny demigods on stilts. . . . Here, the people who compose what is called "society" enjoy even less freedom than their counterparts in Europe. Yet they**

seem unaware of this restriction since their way of life tends to inhibit personality development from childhood.

Ouch, or as they say in Princeton, *Touché!* I can't vouch for the personality bit because I never got that close to an eating club. But "quaint and ceremonious" is spot on.

chapter 12

Predictions
That Time Forgot

Missed Takes

IT DIDN'T BRUSH OFF EASILY

When the French painter Paul Delaroche (1797–1856) saw an exhibition of daguerrotypes in 1839, he announced with magisterial grimness, **"From today painting is dead."** He turned out to be only partly right. His fellow painters, realizing that they could not compete with the new art of photography in its straightforward depiction of the physical world, gradually began to abandon representational art and to create a more personalized, often idiosyncratic modernist mélange. Realism died, but in its wake, as a defensive adaptation to Daguerre's marvel, came Impressionism, Cubism, Abstract Expressionism, and the Photorealism of the late twentieth century.

Photography, for its part, also adapted, reflecting internally the same conflicts about art's identity that necessitated redefinition in the ateliers. Daguerre's precise, almost superrepresentational images were replaced by the impressionistic fuzziness of the Photo-Secession, by the cubist leanness of so-called straight photography, and by such modern games as minimalism and montage. If Delaroche were alive today, he would marvel at the way in which modern technology, far from killing off traditional genres of expression, has helped to reshape and revivify the artistic impulse.

FORD ONLY KNOWS

Given the thoroughness with which the automobile has transformed American society, it's hard to believe that, less than a century ago, the "horseless carriage" was a figure of popular mirth. Check motoring cartoons in the family magazines of the 1900s, or speak to anyone who recalls the spluttering of the early roadsters, and you'll come across, again and again, the prediction of failure. Before World War I, cars seemed to spend more time in ditches than on the road. Flivver owners endured constant ribbing from the horse-and-buggy set, who told them, **"If God had intended man to travel twelve miles an hour, He would have given him wings."** Stranded motorists, their arms weary from cranking, heard over and over the classic piece of advice, **"Get a horse."**

Then along came Ford and his amazingly inexpensive Model T. Advertised as reliable transportation for the masses, it first appeared in 1908, when it sold for just over eight hundred dollars. In the next two decades fifteen million Tin Lizzies rolled off the assembly line, the Sunday drive became an American institution, and our popular culture—from vacations to food to sex—would never be the same again.

WHEN TITANS FALL

Among the ancient Greeks, the philosophical concept known as *hubris* was frequently cited to account for the fall of the high and mighty. *Hubris* meant pride or, more precisely, insolence, and one who displayed it was doomed because the gods would not tolerate a human being, no matter how heroic, who failed to recognize the inherent limitations of mortal life. It's fitting, therefore, that the British luxury liner *Titanic* should have been named for the prideful Titans of Greek mythology. As they fell from heaven, so the liner fell from the sea—a victim, the poetic might say, of overweening confidence.

That confidence hampered the judgment not just of the White

Star Line's owners, who described the vessel as "unsinkable" and who thus neglected to provide its passengers with sufficient lifeboats. It also fouled the thinking of the ship's captain, who allowed his 46,000 ton responsibility to steam rapidly through iceberg-dotted waters. And it even affected the judgment of the nearby *Californian*'s passengers and crew, who saw distress flares from the *Titanic*'s decks but took them to be fireworks.

Just before the fateful voyage began, a *Titanic* deckhand put *hubris* into words. Asked by a passenger whether the company's promotional literature was really accurate, he responded, **"God himself couldn't sink this ship."** If a Greek had heard that, he'd never have gotten on board.

FLY THE UNFRIENDLY SKIES

Because World War I had been fought primarily in the trenches, many military experts of the 1920s believed that future wars would also happen there. An exception was U.S. army officer Billy Mitchell (1879–1936). His advocacy of air power, at the end of the Great War, was so unpopular that he fought for three years for the mere chance to show its effectiveness. He got the chance in 1921, when his superiors let him drop bombs on a captured German battleship to see what damage his novel approach might be able to cause.

Mitchell said airborne bombs would sink the ship. The brass, for the most part, thought he was nuts. Secretary of War Newton Baker, displaying more machismo than prudence, said, **"I'm willing to stand on the bridge of a battleship while that nitwit tries to hit it from the air."** His navy counterpart, Secretary Josephus Daniels, was blunter. Believing Mitchell's dream of air power to be little more than a boyish fantasy, he said, **"Good God! This man should be writing dime novels."** They allowed the experiment, anyway, probably to expose the airman's madness to the newspapers. Within moments, the German battleship was foam on the water.

Billy Mitchell died in 1936. Five years later, on December 7, 1941, the U.S.S. *Arizona* was sent to the bottom by Japanese bombers. Over

1,200 American servicemen died aboard that vessel, proving "crazy" Billy's theory under wartime conditions.

OK, LET'S WORK WITH WHAT YOU'VE GOT

In the 1920s an Omaha-born hoofer named Frederick Austerlitz paired up with his sister, Adele, to perform on the vaudeville circuit. They never attained the superstardom of Georgie Jessel or Al Jolson, but they did well enough to pay the rent and give young Fred the sawdust bug, so when Adele retired toward the end of the decade, he made it to Hollywood and lobbied for a screen test. In 1928, MGM obliged him.

Maybe he was off that day, or maybe the testers were off, but for whatever reason the test was a bust. The man who would personify wit and grace throughout the Depression, who with Ginger Rogers would form the greatest dance duo in American movie history, and whose choreography would win him a special Academy Award—Fred Astaire that day elicited this reaction: **"Can't act. Can't sing. Can dance a little."** The speaker was a studio executive reviewing the test; his name has been, perhaps by his own hand, erased from history.

KING KONG II

William Clark Gable, universally acknowledged as the king of Hollywood in its golden years, was thirty before he made it on the screen. After a decade of acting on Broadway and in road shows, he reached Hollywood in 1930 for a screen test, arranged by a friend from his touring days, Lionel Barrymore. MGM, Barrymore's studio, turned him down. So did Warners, which was then casting for *Little Caesar*. Producer Darryl Zanuck's dismissal is Hollywood legend. After watching Gable try out for the role that would make Edward G. Robinson a star, he sniffed, **"His ears are too big. He looks like an ape."**

Luckily for Gable, MGM reconsidered. In 1931, he was cast as a black hat in the forgettable Western *The Painted Desert*. The next year saw *Red Dust* and *Strange Interlude,* and in 1934 came *It Happened One*

Night, Frank Capra's masterful best picture, which also earned Oscars for Gable and his costar, Claudette Colbert. Ape or not, the king was on his way.

The story makes Zanuck sound like a fool, but in fact he was one of Tinseltown's most successful producers—for two decades the head of Twentieth Century-Fox and the muscle behind such creative and financial winners as *The Grapes of Wrath, All About Eve,* and *The Longest Day.* As the "ears" quote indicates, he was not one to pull his punches. His attitude as studio boss may be summed up in his famous snap at a group of fawning subordinates: **"Don't say yes until I finish talking."**

LEAD SCRATCHES DIAMOND

In his violent life, the gangster Jack Diamond (1895–1931) beat over twenty criminal charges, including several counts of murder and assault, and also survived many attempts on his life. So good was he at eluding both the noose and his fellow racketeers' tommy guns that it was said he had acquired his nickname, "Legs," because of his facility in outrunning doom. In the middle of the Roaring Twenties, with half a dozen slugs already weighing him down, he claimed, much as Napoleon had claimed, **"The bullet hasn't been made that can kill me."**

But he wasn't as lucky as Napoleon. One week before Christmas of 1931, he walked jubilantly out of a courtroom in Troy, New York, having beaten his latest rap, a kidnapping charge. The next day he lay dead in an Albany rooming house, shot in the back of the head by rival goons. The man whom *New York Times* writer Meyer Berger called a **"human ammunition dump for the underworld"** had finally downed one lead snack too many.

IRVING THALBERG, MEET DAVID GRIFFITH

According to the trivia books, when MGM's Louis B. Mayer was thinking about purchasing the rights to *Gone with the Wind* in 1936, Hollywood's "boy wonder," Irving G. Thalberg, stopped him with this classic line, **"Forget it, Louis. No Civil War picture ever made a nickel."** Great story. Little evidence that it's true, however, and to me it sounds like one of those terrific nuggets that get a pedigree simply by repetition.

Thalberg's biographer Bob Thomas, for example, says that Thalberg turned down a shot at *Gone with the Wind* himself because, fresh from producing *Mutiny on the Bounty* and *The Good Earth,* he was tired of making budget-straining epics. Samuel Marx's double memoir *Mayer and Thalberg* doesn't mention the incident at all. Gary Carey's popular biography of Mayer, *All the Stars in Heaven,* does, but only in one of those chatty, no-citation contexts you expect from popular biographies.

If Thalberg did say it, he was displaying an appalling ignorance of his own industry's history. D. W. Griffith's Civil War epic, *The Birth of a Nation* (1915), had practically invented the idea of feature film. It played in the White House to President Wilson's stunned approval, was immediately hailed as a benchmark of cinematic creativity—and broke box office records everywhere it was shown. At an early profit of approximately five million dollars, it made Griffith and his colleagues a hundred million nickels.

NEVILLE'S NOSTRUM

It's ironic that Great Britain's Neville Chamberlain (1869–1940) has gone down in history as the ultimate appeaser, for when he was prime minister (1937–1940) he tried to implement a conservative policy of deterrence through strength. Appeasement was only a stratagem, never a goal. Knowing his country was ill prepared for war, he tried to stall European fascism's territorial expansion while Britain rearmed, hoping that negotiation would keep Hitler and Mussolini in their holes long enough for the British armed forces, devastated by World War I, to gain strength. Thus he gave up Ethiopia to the Italians on Mussolini's promise that he would withdraw from the Spanish Civil War, and surrendered the German portion of Czechoslovakia to the Third Reich on Hitler's promise that this would be his last request.

The latter agreement, the infamous Munich pact, was signed in September 1938, and it is from that agreement that poor old Neville earned his reputation. It's hard to say what he was thinking when he returned from Munich, but what he uttered was the most famous palliative in modern history: "**I believe it is peace in our time.**" This belief rested on Hitler's keeping his word, and he did that for only six months. In March of 1939 his troops took the rest of Czechoslovakia, and on September 1 they invaded Poland. Bitterly aware that appeasement had failed, Chamberlain announced that Britain would aid the Poles, gave up the prime ministry to Winston Churchill, and died in November 1940. "Our time" had lasted eleven months.

TODAY GOLD, TOMORROW THE WORLD

As Franklin Roosevelt's administration grappled with the Depression, even his fabled "brain trust" was sometimes divided over the extent to which the federal government could, or should, fiddle with the economy. The internal dissension was particularly strong in the spring of 1933 when, in an effort to stabilize falling prices, FDR decided to take the country off the gold standard.

Among those supporting the president's decision was the influential columnist Walter Lippman. In an April 18 column in the *Herald Tribune,* he presented his many readers a choice "between keeping up prices at home and keeping up the gold value of the currency abroad." Credit expansion and public works demanded the former—and thus the jettisoning of the "hard money" boys' gold standard. Among the most vocal of the hard money crowd—those who feared inflation more than they did unemployment—were the president's unofficial adviser Bernard Baruch, who warned that only the "debtor class" would profit from the radical measure, and his official budget director, Lewis Douglas, whose prediction was as bitterly sweeping as it was unsound. In an advisers' meeting when it had become clear that FDR's mind was made up, Douglas resigned himself to the inevitable, and glumly announced, "**This is the end of Western civilization.**"

Somehow Western civilization survived gold's banishment, although Douglas himself wasn't quite as lucky. He resigned as budget director in 1934, protesting the unsoundness of New Deal fiscal policy, and began a long and profitable career in private industry.

YOU CAN'T WIN 'EM ALL

Cheryl Crawford (1902–1986) was an extremely savvy New York theater producer who cofounded both the Group Theater and the Actors Studio. Working with Harold Clurman and Lee Strasberg on the first venture, she helped to introduce the Stanislavsky method into the United States and make a sawdust star of playwright Clifford Odets. As a kind of shadow angel on the second, she was distantly responsible for the rise of Brando and Newman—Strasberg controlled the famous training ground in its glory days, but Crawford had been there, with ideas and money, at the beginning.

As an independent producer, she had a knack for spotting gold. Gershwin's *Porgy and Bess* on its original outing (1935) enjoyed only modest success; Crawford's 1942 revival ran twice as long. The following year, she introduced Mary Martin to Broadway in the two-year smash *One Touch of Venus*. Her production of *Brigadoon* ran for 581 nights, and she also backed Tennessee Williams's *Sweet Bird of Youth* and *The Rose Tattoo*.

Crawford was not, however, infallible. Among the properties she turned down were *West Side Story, Who's Afraid of Virginia Woolf?* and *Death of a Salesman*. For the Miller play she could not envision an audience. When her Actors Studio buddy Elia Kazan approached her with the idea, she shook her head: **"Who would want to see a play about an unhappy traveling salesman? Too depressing."** Kazan did it without her, with Lee J. Cobb in the title role, and it became the Pulitzer prize sensation of the 1949 season.

PROMISES, PROMISES

Richard Nixon's relationship with the press resembled that of the Roadrunner with Wile E. Coyote. Or maybe it was the other way around. During most of the Whittier warrior's strange presidency, unless you were a true believer of one or the other side, it was hard to say who was harrying whom. The Nixon camp claimed the press boys had it in for him. Even Watergate, they said, was less an instance of executive malfeasance than a case of the liberal left "hounding" a good man out of office. The Ben Bradlee crowd said it was his own fault. Nixon had isolated himself from honest coverage, not to mention honesty itself, for twenty years; Watergate was merely the chickens coming home to roost.

The funny thing is, Nixon could have avoided the mess of Watergate entirely if he had only kept one famous promise he made to the press. That promise was made in 1962, two years after he lost the White House to John F. Kennedy and only hours after losing the California governor's seat to Edmund Brown. To the journalists who assembled to get his views on this second loss, Nixon grumbled bitterly, **"You won't have Nixon to kick around any more because, gentlemen, this is my last press conference."** That promise turned out to have a six-year half-life. In 1968 a refurbished Nixon was up again, dodging the coyotes, pressing the flesh, and sealing his fate.

THE MIRAGE AT THE END OF THE TUNNEL

One of the most dispiriting aspects of the United States' involvement in Vietnam was that every few months, as the body bag figures continued to mount and the nation became more bitterly divided over administration policy, some bright prognosticator would tell the millions not to worry. The end, he would say reassuringly, was almost in sight. It was the repeated frustration of that promise, as much as the tragedy of the war itself, that convinced increasing numbers of Americans that their government was lost.

The working metaphor in those days for "end in sight" was the proverbial **"light at the end of the tunnel."** Newspaper columnist Stewart Alsop saw it in the fall of 1965. "At last there is light at the end of the tunnel," he wrote, just one year after the Gulf of Tonkin Resolution had authorized the war's first major escalation. President Johnson saw it a year later, announcing that he spied the end of "what has been a long and lonely tunnel." One year after that, the seer was State Department planner Walt Rostow, and in December of 1967, according to David Halberstam's *The Best and the Brightest,* the U.S.

embassy in Saigon had grown so fond of the phrase that it appeared on a New Year's Eve party invitation: "Come see the light at the end of the tunnel." Two months later came the Tet Offensive, and the light which had seemed so close warp-sped away.

WHAT I MEANT WAS...

There is really no very hard evidence that Gerald Ford was, as a joke during his administration had it, **"too dumb to walk and chew gum at the same time."** He did make it through Yale Law, after all (in the top third of his class), and in the late 1960s he led his party in the House. Chances are he had *something* on the ball.

He was responsible, however, for one astonishingly ill-considered executive action—the full pardon, before a trial, of Richard Nixon. And he did, in his 1976 debates with Jimmy Carter, make one remarkably stupid statement about Eastern Europe. Since his party had been fighting the Cold War for thirty years, and since the first and most sensitive battleground of that war was Eastern Europe, it's hard to imagine what, if anything, was in Ford's mind when he let this zinger slip: **"There is no Soviet domination in Eastern Europe, and there never will be under a Ford administration."** It was like a Red Sox fan saying they'd never lost a World Series. Carter pounced on him, of course, and he dug the hole deeper by musing aloud, **"I don't believe the Poles consider themselves dominated by the Soviet Union . . . "** More pouncing, more wriggling, more gasps from GOP headquarters. The election was held two months after this blunder, and Ford *almost* crawled out of the hole, but not quite.

chapter 13

Second Drafts

Updated Quotes

DON'T BET THE RANCH

The author of Ecclesiastes made a sobering refutation of what would later be called social Darwinism when he or she observed, "**The race is not to the swift nor the battle to the strong.**" The idea was that force of circumstance—"time and chance," in the writer's phrasing—could always undo what human endeavor had sought to achieve, and that you should therefore be ever aware of your limitations.

History provides plenty of support for this idea, ranging from such cosmic intercessions as the "Protestant wind" that helped to sink the Spanish Armada to lesser quirks of fate like Leon Spinks becoming heavyweight champion. Essayist Frank Moore Colby put a homey spin on the notion when, in his collection *Constrained Attitudes,* he wrote, "**In public we say the race is to the strongest; in private we know that a lopsided man runs the fastest along the little side-hills of success.**" It's a little hard to visualize that observation, but the idea is clear enough.

Damon Runyon's update was even clearer. The Broadway raconteur, short story writer, and journalist favored no-nonsense punchy prose

146

and lots of slang. He was also known to tout a nag or two, and *his* Ecclesiastes runs true to form. **"The race may not be to the swift or the battle to the strong, but that's the way to bet."**

MR. DOOLEY THREADS THE NEEDLE

In the gospels we find that **"It is easier for a camel to pass through the eye of a needle than for a rich man to enter the kingdom of heaven."** Not great news for the affluent, so it is not surprising that the line was often read metaphorically by pious Gilded Agers who supposed, on very thin evidence, that the "needle" was a narrow gate in the city of Jerusalem. They might have saved themselves the trouble of this queer invention, for the camel/eye image was proverbial in Jesus's time for any great difficulty, and he gives the moneybags an out when he says that with God, all things are possible.

If you've got to correct the original, try Mr. Dooley's version. Martin Dooley, the brogue-and-brickbat-slinging alter ego of American journalist Finley Peter Dunne (1867–1936), filled Chicago papers with his clever archness at the turn of the century. Among his most frequent targets were well-off poseurs and the social inequity that their plutocratic tastes both mirrored and exacerbated. Dunne's edit of the evangelists, from the 1901 book *Mr. Dooley's Opinions,* read as follows: **"Tis as hard f'r a rich man to enther th' kingdom iv Hiven as it is f'r a poor man to get out iv Purgatory."**

THE BOOK OF J. PAUL

"Blessed are the meek, for they shall inherit the earth." That's Jesus, in the Sermon on the Mount. He was referring, presumably, to the post-Apocalypse earth, when as the fundamentalists tell us, *everything* will be different. For this world, I'd go with J. Paul Getty's version. The American billionaire who made his fortune in oil gave the following cynical rewording of the famous line: **"The meek shall inherit the earth, but not its mineral rights."**

RULES GOLDEN AND GILDED

The Golden Rule has worked as a guide to conduct for many centuries and in many cultures. Confucius put it negatively when he advised, **"Whatever you wish not to be done to yourself, do not do that thing to another person."** Jesus phrased it positively, in the Western formula, **"Do unto others as you would have them do unto you."** Immanuel Kant, following Jesus, made the rule of thumb part of his famous Categorical Imperative, suggesting that one test of an action's moral universality is to ask whether or not you'd agree to be the recipient, or object, of the action. The common truth in all these versions is the same: One reliable guide to moral judgment is self-interest.

Post-Kantian writers have amended the observation to humorous effect, and here, as in so many other arenas, it seems the devil has been left with the best lines. Of the more jaundiced approaches to the Golden Rule, I particularly like Edward Noyes Westcott, who in his 1898 novel *David Harum* counsels, **"Do unto the other feller the way he'd like to do unto you an' do it fust."** A more mercantile twist is provided in the plutocratic adage **"He who has the gold, rules."** And as always there is George Bernard Shaw. In his 1903 masterpiece *Man and Superman,* the "maxims for revolutionists" that form part of the play's apparatus include **"Do not do unto others as you would that they should do unto you. Their tastes may not be the same"** and the curt, self-referential paradox **"The Golden Rule is that there are no golden rules."**

CASH OR CHARGE?

"In God we trust" was an English slogan years before it was first printed on American money. That happened in 1864, when the Union had good cause to look to Providence. But it wasn't until almost a century later—in 1956—that Congress made it the official national motto. My favorite update of the line is the merchant's warning that you sometimes see in down-home establishments: **"In God we trust. All others pay cash."** A similar sense of vendor's caution is reflected in the liquor store announcement, **"We have come to an understanding with the local banks. They don't sell beer and we don't cash checks."**

PUFFING, SPARTAN STYLE

Before he became Rome's "dictator for life" in 44 B.C., Julius Caesar had to defeat his principal rival for the honor, Pompey, in a civil war that lasted three years. After his easternmost victory in that conflict, the 47 B.C. defeat of Pompey's ally Pharnaces at Zela, Caesar announced his success in the terse boast *"Veni, vidi, vici,"* or **"I came, I saw, I conquered."** A classic bit of military folklore, the phrase is also useful as a litmus test separating the two main camps of Latin scholars: The so-called classically trained pronounce it "Way-knee, wee-dee, wee-kee," while the church trained say "Vay-knee, vee-dee, vee-chee."

The line was updated most recently during the 1991 Gulf War, when flag wavers' bumper stickers matched Caesar's hubris with the line **"We came, we saw, we kicked ass."** A less jingoistic modification is the pseudo-ad *"Veni, vidi, Visa,"* which translates roughly as **"I came, I saw, I shopped."**

GRACE NOTES

John Bradford (1510–1555) was one of the Protestants who died for their faith under Mary Tudor, England's famous "Bloody Mary" of popular legend. A pious and gentle man, he went to the stake calmly, telling a fellow victim as they were about to be burned, **"We shall have a merry supper with the Lord this night."** That line alone would be enough to ensure him epigrammatic immortality, but he had another that was even better known. Seeing a criminal on the way to his execution, Bradford remarked, **"There but for the grace of God goes John Bradford."** Substitute "go I" for the last three words and you've got one of the commonest expressions of humility in the English language.

It's been neatly twisted to humorous intent in our secular age, with the identity of the speaker varying depending on the source. Some say the updated version was first given by Winston Churchill as an aside on his fellow statesman Sir Stafford Cripps. Others—the majority—say it was writer Herman Mankiewicz, coauthor of *Citizen Kane,* and that the target of the line was boy wonder Orson Welles. Whoever started it, the modern version runs like this: **"There but for the grace of God goes God."**

GIVING SHORT SHIFT

"Brevity is the soul of wit," said Shakespeare's Hamlet, so I'll keep this one short. Dorothy Parker, during her time at *Vanity Fair* magazine, was once asked to come up with caption copy for a feature spread on ladies' undergarments. Her submission: **"Brevity is the soul of lingerie."**

ALL THESE ROUGHNESSES

During the 1988 presidential campaign, candidate George Bush claimed that he was offering himself to the American public as Abraham Lincoln had offered himself, not gussied up to appear more presentable but with his drawbacks clearly visible, **"warts and all."** His invocation of Lincoln was a standard GOP campaign ploy, but his citation of the great man was erroneous. It wasn't Lincoln, but the English rebel statesman Oliver Cromwell, who wanted the public to appraise him "warts and all."

When the English Civil War broke in the 1640s over the relative powers of Parliament and the Crown, Cromwell quickly became a military leader of the Parliamentary faction. Although initially he had no interest in abolishing the monarchy, the intransigence of Charles I made accommodation difficult, and Cromwell eventually stood among those who approved his execution in January of 1649. A little less than five years later, with a string of field victories serving as qualifications, he became Lord Protector of the realm. Holding that supreme office until his death in 1658, he ruled England with Puritan principles and personal magnetism, implementing tolerance in both religious and judicial matters that was remarkably advanced for the Europe of his time.

His "warts and all" comment was made to the popular court painter Peter Lely, who did Cromwell's portrait just before he became Protector. According to Horace Walpole's *Anecdotes of Painting in England* (1762), he told Lely, "**I desire you would use all your skill to paint my picture truly like me, and not flatter me at all; but remark all these roughnesses, pimples, warts, and everything as you see me, otherwise I will never pay a farthing for it.**" As far as we know, Lely followed his direction, although it may have given him a lasting distaste for such realism: After the Restoration replaced Cromwell's regime, he specialized in flattering portraits of court ladies.

THE LONG AND THE SHORT OF IT

After years of presiding over Princeton University, Woodrow Wilson's first foray into politics came when he became governor, in 1910, of the Garden State. Two New Jerseyans who heard him speak as governor gave him material for one of his favorite stories. They were equally impressed with the speaker's obvious intelligence, but to one it was also something of a mystery. "**What I don't see,**" he told his friend, "**is what a fellow as smart as that was doing hanging around a college so long.**"

Wilson's speeches, both in New Jersey and beyond, grabbed his audiences not because of his natural intelligence—or because of that long Princeton tenure—but because, like every successful writer, he worked on them, word by word, until they sang. When one of his cabinet asked him how long it typically took him to prepare a speech, Wilson said it depended on the podium time. "**If I am to speak ten minutes, I need a week for preparation. If fifteen minutes, three days. If half an hour, two days. If an hour, I am ready now.**"

The cleverness of this rule of thumb is exceeded only by its deadpan accuracy. Thoreau made a similar point in 1857, when he wrote a friend that a story he was considering need not be long, but that **"it will take a long while to make it short."** Exactly two centuries before that, in his *Lettres Provinciales* of 1657, the French philosopher Blaise Pascal wrote the line that underlay both Thoreau's and Wilson's observations. **"I have made this letter long,"** he said, **"only because I lacked the time to make it short."**

THE ENEMY WITHIN

Two Perry boys figure prominently in U.S. naval history. Commodore Matthew Perry was responsible, in the 1850s, for opening up reluctant Japan to U.S. trade. His elder brother Oliver Hazard Perry commanded the U.S. fleet at the Battle of Lake Erie, an 1813 engagement that gave the Americans control of the Ohio Valley and forced the British Navy, for the first time in its history, to surrender a squadron. Perry's postbattle announcement to army commander William Henry Harrison became a staple of U.S. military legend: **"We have met the enemy and they are ours."**

In World War II, U.S. airman David Mason equalled the laconic precision of Perry's report when he radioed back to his base the four-word message **"Sighted sub. Sank same."** Another twist on the Perry line came during the Vietnam War period. Reacting to the confusion and soul searching surrounding U.S. involvement, Walt Kelly's Pogo remarked ruefully, **"We have met the enemy and he is us."**

OUR COUNTRY: RIGHT, WRONG, OR REFORMABLE

During the Vietnam War and to a lesser degree during Desert Storm, gung-ho supporters of U.S. presidential policy frequently reacted to public dissent with a sense of outrage. When you're at war, the proadministration consensus seemed to go, you must put up a united front for outside parties, lest the appearance of dissension undermine the national cause.

In American history, the classic statement of this type of patriotism was made by naval hero Stephen Decatur, at an 1815 fete honoring his exploits. Decatur had just returned from the second of two tours in the Mediterranean, where he had succeeded in suppressing attacks on American vessels and forcing a treaty on the perennially obnoxious Barbary pirates. Responding to a toast at a Norfolk, Virginia, dinner, Decatur raised his glass with the following words: "**Our country. In her intercourse with foreign nations may she always be in the right. But our country, right or wrong.**"

A noble sentiment, but as many commentators have pointed out, it's also an invitation to confuse the "country" with the gang in power. That's not necessarily the most intelligent, or even the most patriotic, approach to policy. That's probably why Winston Churchill, in a 1947 Commons speech, echoed Decatur's sentiment with an important rider: "**When I am abroad,**" he said, "**I make it a rule never to criticize or attack the government of my own country. I make up for lost time when I come home.**" Why the American reformer Carl Schurz amended the hero's point by saying "**When wrong, to be made right.**" And why the English writer G. K. Chesterton winked maliciously, "**My country right or wrong . . . is like saying: My mother drunk or sober.**"

KILLJOY WAS HERE

Percy Shelley's bitter lyric "Ozymandias" reflects on the vanity of human endeavor by describing the ruined tomb of an ancient Egyptian king. All that remains of the once renowned monarch's mark on the earth are "two vast and trunkless legs of stone," a "shattered visage," and a pedestal on which the king, Ozymandias, exhorts the viewer, "Look on my works, ye Mighty, and despair!" Shelley ends the poem thus:

> **Nothing beside remains. Round the decay**
> **Of that colossal wreck, boundless and bare**
> **The lone and level sands stretch far away.**

A century after the English poet's death, Morris Bishop, a Cornell professor who wrote light verse for the *New Yorker* in the 1940s and 1950s, amended the sobering observation in his little gem "Ozymandias

Revisited." The focus here is on the insult that tourists add to injury when, emulating the royal vanity, they compound the weather of time with modern graffiti. In his poem, which appeared in the 1942 collection *Spilt Milk,* Bishop copies Shelley's opening lines, then concludes:

> And on the pedestal these words appear:
> "My name is Ozymandias, king of kings:
> Look on my works, ye Mighty, and despair!"
> Also the names of Emory P. Gray,
> Mr. and Mrs. Dukes, and Oscar Baer
> Of 17 West 4th St., Oyster Bay.

To the reading public, this quote was (and is) a typical product of the Bishop pen. His colleagues also knew him as an indefatigable essayist, covering subjects as diverse as Dante, Nabokov, the Norman Conquest, literary usage, and the history of Cornell. Humorist Frank Sullivan, who had been his classmate in Ithaca early in the century, confessed that when he viewed Bishop's accomplishments, "**I am forced to the conclusion that in addition to his talent he has been privately blessed with a twenty-eight-hour day.**"

WHOSE MOUSETRAP?

One of the more literary expressions of the free market faith goes like this. "**If a man write a better book, preach a better sermon, or make a better mousetrap than his neighbor, though he build his house in the woods, the world will make a beaten path to his door.**" That's the way the thought is given in the standard quotation collections, where it's usually attributed to Ralph Waldo Emerson. The American businessman and author Elbert Hubbard also claimed it, however, suggesting that Sarah Yule, who credits it to Emerson in her book *Borrowings* (1889), actually got it from one of his (Hubbard's) lectures. No one will ever know for sure where Mrs. Yule picked it up. What's certain is its durability as a capitalist catchphrase. With a memorable image and verbal economy, it sums up Adam Smith's fundamental observation that, in a free market, the "best" products will win the day.

That's the theory, anyway. In the age of planned obsolescence, junk food, and million-dollar ad budgets, Smith's sanguinity is a little hard to swallow. You don't need to be a severe critic of modern capitalism to recognize that marketing, rather than product excellence, is the name of today's game, and that when a "better" hamburger or compact disc or compact car finds its way into Mr. and Mrs. Consumer's home, it's because the producer, in thirty-second spots, has done the path beating.

Becoming a successful producer, however, has its down side, one which writer Newman Levy predicted a half-century ago. Writing in H. L. Mencken's *American Mercury* in 1935, Levy reassessed the mousetrap notion with acerbic wit:

> **If a man builds a better mousetrap than his neighbor, the world will not only beat a path to his door, it will make newsreels of him and his wife in beach pajamas, it will discuss his diet and his health, it will publish heartthrob stories of his love life, it will publicize him, analyze him, photograph him, and make his life thoroughly miserable by feeding to the palpitant public intimate details of things that are none of its damned business.**

That's a comment on the fledgling tabloidists of the 1930s. You can imagine what Levy would have said about the *National Enquirer*.

CHOICE JOYCE

I have a special affection for Joyce Kilmer. We were born in the same town in New Jersey, and as a child I played frequently beneath the oak that local legend says inspired his poem "Trees." Up until recently, many American children knew the poem by heart, and took pleasure in fulsome mimicry of its opening lines:

> **I think that I shall never see**
> **A poem lovely as a tree.**

It's a pity that Kilmer should be remembered for this rather insipid nature piece, for he wrote fine battle poetry during World War I before falling himself in France in 1918. That's forgotten today, thanks to *Poetry* magazine, which featured "Trees" in its August 1913 issue, turning its author into the patron saint of newspaper verse.

Of the numerous parodies of "Trees" that have been churned out in the past eight decades, I still like Ogden Nash's best. The premier American exponent of "light verse," Nash responded to Joyce's naturism with the mock-bucolic quatrain "Song of the Open Road":

> **I think that I shall never see**
> **A billboard lovely as a tree.**
> **Indeed, unless the billboards fall**
> **I'll never see a tree at all.**

BICENTENNIAL BOFFO

Nobody ever accused Gerald Ford of wittiness, but on at least one occasion he had, as the English say, some "good innings." It was during the not-so-great debates between him and Jimmy Carter, the Georgia peanut tycoon who became the Democrats' surprise candidate in 1976.

In that bicentennial year, the republic was in a pretty parlous state, spiritually speaking, what with the stain of Watergate still clinging to the GOP, South Vietnam and Cambodia both fallen to the Communists, and the sitting president, a beacon of amiability in a rough world, bearing the cross of having merely inherited the Oval Office. Carter, no slouch at amiability himself, soft-pedaled the Watergate connection and even the notorious pardon that Ford had granted to his outgoing predecessor. But soft-pedal or no, he was obviously offering a new moral deal. A plain-spoken, Baptist man-of-the-soil (even if he was worth millions), he tried his best to bring "morality" back in style, and it was the pious pitch, in all likelihood, that got him the presidency.

For a Realpolitik Republican, even one as candy-coated as Jerry Ford, you didn't deal with the Russkies and other villains by preaching the Word. Painting Carter as potentially a weak-kneed disaster, he got off one of the best lines of the debate when he put a twisted version of Teddy-boyism into Carter's mouth. Teddy Roosevelt, Ford reminded the audience, had advised the nation to speak softly and carry a big stick—advice Ford himself had taken the year before, when he retook the U.S. freighter *Mayaguez* from Cambodian captors. As for his opponent, **"Jimmy Carter wants to speak loudly and carry a fly swatter."**

STUDY WAR NO MORE

Prairie poet Carl Sandburg (1878–1967) is usually credited with originating the image of an unattended war in his most famous celebration of democracy, "The People, Yes." In that 1936 poem, he wrote **"Someday they'll give a war and nobody will come."** The idea was reproduced with a tentative slant on thousands of Vietnam-era bumper stickers: **"What if they gave a war and nobody came?"** A final, politically more astute version appeared in the Reagan years, when domestic budget cuts were widely blamed on military excess: **"Won't it be nice when the schools all have enough money and the Pentagon has to hold a bake sale to pay for a bomber?"**

ARE WE HAVING FUN YET?

The glass and steel boxes that urban professionals work in today are the legacy of the so-called International Style of architecture, that squeaky clean child of the German Bauhaus, which by the 1950s had become *the* style of corporate construction. Its aesthetic, as lean and mean as its materials, was supposed to promote efficiency without clutter. Its most famous practitioner, former Bauhaus head Ludwig Mies van der Rohe, summed up his intention economically: **"Less is more."**

This minimalist approach to design conquered the century, but in recent years has begun to lose ground. The Internationalists' chief antagonists, the Postmodernists, have fostered a whimsical resurgence of both surface and internal ornament. As Mannerism thumbed its nose at Renaissance ideas of order, so the Postmodernists have looked at the sheer façade of the modern skyscraper, taken out pots of Day-Glo, and started hurling. A glass-and-steel structure with a Greek pediment at the top and a sideshow barker in the lobby—that's an example of the quirky mélanges the new school loves.

The chief Postmodernist theoretician is Robert Venturi, whose buildings are humorous hodgepodges of symbol and form, and whose manifesto, *Complexity and Contradiction in Architecture,* argues for eclecticism and pop culture gaucheness as replacements for austerity. Among Venturi's many jabs at corporate plainness, I like especially his archly smiling estimate that "**Main Street is almost all right**" and his self-conscious parody of the Miesian commandment, "**Less is a bore.**"

"PROPERTY": WHATEVER I WANT

You want an instant snapshot of the difference between the 1960s and what came after? The 1960s, which gave us "**It's cool**" and "**Whatever turns you on**" and "**Let it be,**" also gave us pop guru Jesse Lair's wonderfully flaccid ode to self-determination. From his 1974 book *I Ain't Much, Baby, But I'm All I Got,* it goes like this:

> **If you want something very very badly,**
> **let it go free. If it comes back to you**
> **it's yours forever. If it doesn't, it was**
> **never yours to begin with.**

That's the laid-back, go-with-the-flow 1960s. Here's an update from the 1980s:

> **If you want something very very badly,**
> **let it go free. If it doesn't come back**
> **to you, hunt it down and kill it.**

Yeah, I *know* it's a joke. A joke that just happens to coincide with increasing levels of domestic violence and international terrorism.

chapter 14

The Fab
Four

A Quartet of Quipsters

THE WINKING VICAR OF ST. PAUL'S

Sydney Smith (1771–1845)

The Reverend Sydney Smith was, as Hamlet says of Yorick, "**a fellow of infinite jest, of most excellent fancy.**" He was also one of the most versatile men of his time. Preacher, editor, judge, doctor, political activist, even builder—Smith took on all of these diverse occupations, not only excelling in them, but delighting everyone he met on the way with his wit and kindness.

The second of five clever and argumentative children, young Smith was so accomplished a scholar that his public school chums refused to compete with him for prizes. He entered Winchester, then Oxford, and finally the ministry, becoming ordained in 1794. He spent the next decade mostly in Edinburgh, where he tutored a young aristocrat, preached what a fellow cleric called "sublime" sermons, and helped to found the *Edinburgh Review*. To that journal he contributed scores of articles over the years. Moving to London around 1803, he distinguished himself as a "fresh and racy" lecturer, an ardent Whig, and an opponent of civil restrictions on Catholics' rights. This last achievement brought him fame as the author of the proemancipation *Letters of Peter Plymley* (1807), but it sat so poorly with his hierarchy that they banished him, in effect, to a country vicarage.

He took it well. He built his own parsonage in the village of Foston, learned farming and horse breeding, served as village magistrate and physician as well as preacher, and continued to speak out on religious discrimination, poor relief, and suffrage reform. When the House of Lords opposed the latter, he likened them to an old lady bucking the ocean. In all of this, he maintained a sunny mien, achieving a judicial reputation, for example, for "making up quarrels and treating poachers gently."

Geniality also informed his conversation, and it was for casual chatter that he became best known. In 1831 he was made canon of St. Paul's, which afforded London, rather than merely Foston, the pleasure of his company. The city took to him as it had taken to Dr. Johnson, though less timidly, for Smith's wit was as cheerful as Johnson's had been cantankerous. **"You flavor everything,"** he once told an acquaintance. **"You are the vanilla of society."** About a pedant he gently remarked, **"He not only overflowed with learning. He stood in the slop."** And about his fellow *Edinburgh Review* founder Francis Jeffrey, he once claimed in mock horror, **"Why, I heard him speak disrespectfully of the equator."**

His time in Scotland afforded him much grist for merriment. Although the Scots and he got along fine, he chided them theatrically for their supposed dullness. **"It requires a surgical operation to get a joke well into a Scotch understanding,"** he said. **"Their only idea of wit . . . is laughing immoderately at stated intervals."** Switzerland he called **"an inferior sort of Scotland,"** while the tongue-in-cheek motto that he proposed for the *Edinburgh Review*—in Latin, of course—translated as **"We cultivate literature upon a little oatmeal."**

His rustic exile also gave him fodder. Country living, he said, was **"a healthy kind of grave . . . I always fear that creation will expire before teatime."** That *would* have been a tragedy, for food was much on the good parson's mind. He was very interested in the problem of hunger among the poor, and twitted the gluttonous in a couple of charming asides. One man's idea of heaven, he said, was **"eating pâté de foie gras to the sound of trumpets."** To a woman who had professed a distaste for sauces: **"Madam, I have been looking for a person who disliked gravy all my life. Let us swear eternal friendship."**

Smith's most frequent target was the established church—and the idiosyncracies that a parson's life necessarily entailed. **"What a pity it is,"** he remarked about his native land, **"that we have no amusements in England but vice and religion."** He enjoyed entwining the two to humorous effect, as in his observation about the episcopacy: **"How can a bishop marry? How can he flirt? The most he can say is, 'I will see you in the vestry after service.'"** Married himself to the same woman for forty-five years, he had enough familiarity with sex to father four children, yet he smiled, **"There are three sexes: men, women, and clergymen."**

Proclaiming his "one illusion" to be the Archbishop of Canterbury, Smith still sniped at his immediate bosses with glib abandon. When church members proposed a wooden walk be laid around St. Paul's, Smith agreed: **"Let the Dean and Canons lay their heads together and the thing will be done."** Parishioners, too, became the victims of his raillery. Of one, Smith decided that he deserved to be **"preached to death by wild curates."** To another, he gave this farewell on his way to the cathedral: **"I am just going to pray for you at St. Paul's, but with no very lively hope of success."**

Most satire is a little cruel. Not Smith's. Being twitted by him must have been like being touched by a Plains Indian coup stick: You felt silly, but there wasn't any blood. One Lord Dudley, a target of Smith's humor for years, claimed he never resented a word that the curate said. That's the true test of the world's Yoricks, those best of fools.

PITY ME, SATAN

Abrose Bierce (1842–?1913)

The peculiar bite of Ambrose Bierce's writing probably comes from the fact that he was as unhappy in love as he was in war. Born in 1842, he joined the Union Army in the Civil War, fought honorably at Shiloh, Chickamauga, and Kennesaw Mountain (where he was wounded), yet was so disheartened by the war's brutality that he refused the government's postwar offer of back pay. Married in 1871 to mining heiress Mary Ellen Day, he lasted four years in Europe on her father's wedding gift—a cool ten grand—but became increasingly bitter about the arrangement upon their return to the United States. Although they weren't divorced until 1904, Bierce thought of marriage, to judge from his writing, as mutual slavery.

Professionally he did all right. A friend of Bret Harte and Mark Twain, he tickled San Francisco newspaper readers in the 1880s and 1890s with epigrams and literary gossip in his column "The Prattler." His sardonic sketches and weird tales filled several volumes, of which the most famous were *In the Midst of Life* and *Can Such Things Be?* In his best-known story, "An Occurrence at Owl Creek Bridge," a young soldier about to be hanged for desertion imagines his escape so realistically that the reader takes it for fact—until, in the last line of the story, he's hanged for real. Bierce's fiction prickles with similar victims and gruesome trick endings.

His reputation as an epigrammatist rests primarily on a caustic dictionary that came out two years after his divorce, in 1906. Originally called *The Cynic's Word Book,* it became *The Devil's Dictionary* in 1911, just two years before its world-weary author disappeared forever into Mexico, supposedly searching for the rebel Pancho Villa. Some idea of the book's disenchanted cleverness may be gained from the following selections:

Auctioneer.   The man who proclaims with a hammer that he has picked a pocket with his tongue.

Beauty.   The power by which a woman charms a lover and terrifies a husband.

Bore.   A person who talks when you wish him to listen.

Brute.   See **Husband.**

Conservative.   A statesman who is enamored of existing evils, as distinguished from the Liberal, who wishes to replace them with others.

Cynic. A blackguard whose faulty vision sees things as they are, not as they ought to be.

Egotist. A person of low taste, more interested in himself than in me.

Future. That period of time in which our affairs prosper, our friends are true, and our happiness is assured.

History. An account mostly false of events most unimportant which are brought about by rulers mostly knaves and soldiers mostly fools.

Impunity. Wealth.

Liar. A lawyer with a roving commission.

Noncombatant. A dead Quaker.

Novel. A short story padded.

Plebescite. A popular vote to ascertain the will of the sovereign.

Politeness. The most acceptable hypocrisy.

Realism. The art of depicting nature as it is seen by toads.

Scribbler. A professional writer whose views are antagonistic to one's own.

Un-American. Wicked, intolerable, heathenish.

Vote. The instrument and symbol of a freeman's power to make a fool of himself and a wreck of his country.

Year. A period of three hundred and sixty-five disappointments.

THE SAGE OF ROYCROFT

Elbert Hubbard (1856–1915)

Elbert Hubbard's personal motto might well have been the Nike Company's advertising slogan **"Just do it."** Like most businessmen of his time, he was convinced that with personal integrity and pluck anyone could lift himself out of anonymity to rival Horatio Alger's heroes as a self-made man. He was his own best proof of this proposition. After leaving high school in his native Illinois, he worked free-lance for a Chicago newspaper, then as a salesman and ad writer for a Buffalo soap company until, by the age of thirty-six, he had socked away enough money to retire.

A brief stint at Harvard convinced Hubbard he had outgrown
higher education, so he went to Europe. There he ran across the head
of the English arts and crafts movement, William Morris, and his life
took a dramatic turn toward the artistic. Impressed by Morris's medi-
evalism and dedication to craftsmanship, he opened a cottage industry
called the Roycroft Shop in upstate New York, where employees turned
out pottery, metal, and leather work, and The Philistine, a monthly
magazine filled with Hubbard's inspirational musings. This literary soap
sold even better than the ashes and lye variety, and by the turn of the
century the former salesman, now styling himself "Fra Elbertus," was
pulling in subscribers' fees from over 200,000 readers—not counting
the honoraria from his popular lecture tours.

The pluck whose material value he had thus twice demonstrated
was immortalized in what became his biggest seller, the 1899 account
of a Spanish-American War hero who overcomes huge odds to bring
"A Message to Garcia." If you think of In Search of Excellence as a business
best-seller, consider this: So many firms bought Hubbard's "Message"
of determination as required reading for their employees that sales
eventually topped forty million.

In The Philistine, in its successor, The Fra, in fourteen volumes of
"Little Journeys" to the homes of famous people, and in sundry collections of essays and epigrams, Hubbard pushed his rosy philosophy of
self-reliance yet peppered it with enough snaps at established authority
that he gained, astonishingly, a reputation for radical thought. He en-
couraged this by copying the dress of the English decadents—flop hat,
curls, big bow ties—and by a literary style that is Wilde gone slightly
flat. He delighted in the epigram, and although his efforts at the form
lacked the bite of Irish whimsy, he did enough of them to fill a volume
of 1001 examples (1911). Of these, even the worst are full of horse
sense, while the best show a dry bohemianism that explains his fame.

On success and its handmaid, money, he was unabashedly bullish.
"All that glitters is not brass," he proclaimed. **"The soldier and
the priest have wrecked every land where they have had the
power—let's give the businessman a chance to build things
up."** He was acutely aware that the way to the top could be fraught
with reverses: **"He who has never made a fool of himself is not**

in my class." Yet he believed, with the innocent faith of his generation, that making it meant picking yourself up and trying again. **"The greatest mistake you can make in life,"** he claimed, was to be **"continually fearing that you will make one."** His definition of *failure* reinforced the point: **"A man who has blundered but is not able to cash in the experience."**

Like many self-made men, he was consistently critical of the pretensions of "college boys." Calling diplomas "certificates" rather than evidence of real learning, he amended the "horse to water" proverb to read **"You can lead a boy to college, but you cannot make him think."** About the Greek Titan who allowed Hercules to trick him into picking up the world after he had laid it down, Hubbard wrote, **"There is every reason to believe that Atlas was a college graduate who had just received his degree."**

"Fra Elbertus" reserved a special disdain for religion, or rather for the lockstep religion of orthodoxy—which he called **"spiritual constipation"** and **"a corpse that doesn't know it's dead."** It was on this ground, probably, that he earned his "radical" reputation, and yet a survey of his sayings suggests he was anything but impious. It was just that his religion was out of step—a kind of late Transcendentalist love for natural possibility, necessarily at odds with creeds or established hierarchies. **"God looked upon His work and saw that it was good. That is where the clergy take issue with Him."** That's as good a capsule of his faith as any, although he also consistently championed the "moral" life, not only as a means to perfection in itself, but also as an ennobling purgatory, a honing of one's individuality, and (not least of all) a model for those who would make a better world. Thus **"We are not punished for our sins, but by them," "God will not look you over for medals, degrees, or diplomas, but for scars,"** and **"Would you make better men? Set them an example."**

Hubbard also had a mildly cynical, world-weary side, which he seems to have adopted from the Wilde-Morris crowd without much enthusiasm. Consider **"The graveyards are full of people the world could not do without."** Or the definition of *experience* as **"the name everyone gives to his mistakes."** Or the Wildean throwaway **"Only**

the shallow know themselves." For the most part, though, he was straight on and kinkily sanguine. He wanted life to work, thought it could if you sweated enough, and was as righteous, in his own way, as any cleric. His most typical advice might be the pedestrian line "**Live each day so as to shake hands with yourself every night.**" Wilde could never have written that—which is to Hubbard's credit.

He was a go-getter with an absolutely unique style. En route to England in 1915, he went down with the torpedoed liner *Lusitania.* Before it sank, he called out to a friend, "**So long, Jack. They're a damn sight worse than I gave them credit for.**"

THE DARK ANGEL OF THE ALGONQUIN

Dorothy Parker (1893–1967)

A father and stepmother she despised. A Jewish surname and a Catholic education. A weakness for strong drink, lost causes, and tepid men. One abortion, two suicide attempts, and more sad affairs than you can shake a swizzle stick at. All masked by an air of ennui and a flair for sarcasm. It sounds like the dreary essentials of a Joan Crawford part. It was Dorothy Parker's life.

Born Dorothy Rothschild to a garment dealer, she was sent to a convent school by her stepmother, lived alone in a Broadway boarding house in her early twenties, married and later divorced stockbroker Edwin Parker, and became drama critic of the old *Vanity Fair.* There she befriended writers Robert Sherwood and Robert Benchley, who brought her into the glittering gabfest that became known, in the 1920s, as the Algonquin Round Table. The group's undisputed diva, Parker was as confident there as she was at sea in her private life. As solid a writer as she was in conventional genres—her story "Big Blonde" won the 1929 O. Henry Prize—she shone best as a cocktail-balancing party brat, and many of the one-liners for which she is remembered first bubbled out in the Algonquin's showy shadows.

Many also found their way into print. A famous couplet on nearsightedness, "News Item," explained why she was loath to correct her vision:

Men seldom make passes
At girls who wear glasses.

Equally memorable was her bittersweet reflection on suicide, published as the poem "Resume":

Razors pain you, rivers are damp.
Acids stain you and drugs cause cramp.
Guns aren't lawful, nooses give.
Gas smells awful. You might as well live.

She also injected numerous acid bon mots into the reviews she wrote for the *New Yorker*. Her most famous dig is probably her assessment of an early Katharine Hepburn play: "**She ran the gamut of emotions from A to B.**" Writing as "Constant Reader," she dismissed one book by saying, "**This is not a novel to be tossed aside lightly. It should be thrown with great force.**" On the interminable memoirs of an English countess, Margot Asquith, she commented, "**The affair between Margot Asquith and Margot Asquith will live as one of the prettiest love stories in all literature.**" And to the sticky sweetness of A. A. Milne's *House at Pooh Corner* she reacted, "**Tonstant Weader Fwowed Up.**"

Politically leftist, Parker defended anarchists Sacco and Vanzetti before their 1927 execution, took constant potshots at the Smart Set who paid her bar bills, and covered the Spanish Civil War for the Communist *New Masses*. It was probably partly politics and partly professional rivalry that led to her famous snaps at Connecticut Republican Clare Boothe Luce. The wife of *Time* magazine founder Henry Luce and a successful playwright before entering Congress, Luce once approached a doorway at the same time as the Algonquin charmer. "**Age before beauty,**" she said, stepping aside. Parker swept in, smiling, "**Pearls**

before swine." On another occasion, a mutual friend defended Luce, claiming that she was always kind to her inferiors. "**Where does she find them?**" asked Parker.

Parker's feminist champions have suggested that her digs at society women are typically tempered with compassion, and that her true subject was the crippling nature of social life. That's a subtle reading, and possibly a sound one, but what comes out in the most memorable of her barbs is a relish in creating parodies of the "loose woman." About a woman who had broken her leg while vacationing in London, she said, "**She probably did it sliding down a barrister.**" On a polyglot party guest: "**She speaks eighteen languages and can't say no in any of them.**" On the coed dates at a Yale prom: "**If all those sweet young things were laid end to end . . . I wouldn't be a bit surprised.**" Most tellingly, perhaps, on herself, when asked if she had enjoyed a certain party: "**Enjoyed it! One more drink and I'd have been under the host.**"

At her peak in the interwar years, she worked on Hollywood screenplays with her second husband, Alan Campbell, helped her friend Lillian Hellman with the dialogue of *Little Foxes,* wrote some Broadway flops, and pumped her corrosive irony into volumes of fiction and poetry. By the fifties, as a sometime contributor to *Esquire,* she had attained the unenviable status of "used to be famous." At her death, her husband having preceded her by four years, she willed most of her estate to Martin Luther King, Jr. Among her best quips are the lines she suggested for her headstone: "**Excuse my dust**" and "**This is on me.**"

chapter 15

What's It All About, Alfie?

Life

WISDOM 101

By scholarly consensus, Isaac Newton was not only the most brilliant mind of his age but also one of the three or four obvious geniuses our species has yet produced. Home on an enforced holiday from plague-ridden Cambridge, he whiled away his time by inventing calculus. His treatise *Opticks* (1704) virtually founded that scientific discipline. In his most famous work, the vast *Principia,* he presented the natural laws of motion and gravitational attraction, which explained the workings of the physical universe until the advent of Einstein. His younger contemporary Alexander Pope was hyperbolic but not counter to the spirit of a thankful age when he wrote

Nature and Nature's laws lay hid in night.
God said, "Let Newton be!" and all was light.

Newton's own estimation of his achievement, however, echoes Socrates's insight that the beginning of wisdom is a sense of your own ignorance. Legend says that the Greek philosopher accounted himself the stupidest of men, and Newton matched him in plangent self-effacement. We find him saying in Brewster's *Memoirs of Newton,* **"I do not know what I may appear to the world but to myself I seem to have been only like a boy playing on the seashore, and diverting myself in now and then finding a smoother pebble or a prettier shell than ordinary, whilst the great ocean of truth lay all undiscovered before me."** Compare that to Oscar Wilde's quip at New York customs that **"I have nothing to declare but my genius,"** and you will see the difference between insight and ingenuity.

IN THE WINK OF AN EYE

Practically everyone who has ever commented on human life has made mention, sometimes lugubriously, sometimes flippantly, of its shortness. Few have done so more vividly than the Benedictine scholar Saint Bede (ca. 672–735), known since the ninth century as the Venerable Bede. He wrote lucidly on numerous subjects, including grammar, theology, and science, but is best known for his *Ecclesiastical History of the English People,* completed in 731. In that book, still a critical source for historians, Bede compares the earthly part of human existence to the flitting of a bird through a king's dining hall. He says that the "present life of man" resembles:

> the flight of a sparrow through the room where you dine in winter, with your commanders and ministers and a good fire in the middle, while rain and snow prevail outside. The sparrow, flying in at one door and immediately out at another, is safe inside from the storm, but after a moment of fair weather, quickly vanishes from sight into the darkness from which it emerged. So this life of man appears for a short span, but of what preceded it, or what is to follow it, we are totally ignorant.

Bede's faith, of course, was that it was better "outside," since that was, theologically speaking, God's country. But the feeling of doubt here is unmistakable, and fully sobering.

PLAYING IT BY EAR

Only an incurable optimist would deny that life proceeds not straightforwardly but in fits and starts. No matter how well you plot the course, half the time you end up somewhere you didn't even know existed because, as Robert Burns put it in his poem "To a Mouse," **"The best laid schemes o' mice and men/Gang aft a-gley."** The Victorian writer Samuel Butler (1835–1902) commented sensibly on this hard reality, once in his *Notebooks* and once in his collected *Essays.* In the *Notebooks,* he is abstractly philosophical, since he believes that people need to get on with it—to keep moving forward and making decisions even though they lack the data to do so confidently. Butler defines life here as **"the art of drawing sufficient conclusions from insufficient premises."** In the *Essays,* he's more pictorial, using a musical analogy to suggest our necessarily improvisational approach to experience: **"Life is like playing a violin solo in public and learning the instrument as one goes on."**

NOTHING SERIOUS

The British poet and dramatist John Gay (1685–1732) wrote widely in the sophisticated couplets of his generation, but was best known for his satirical musical *The Beggar's Opera,* which opened in London in January of 1728 and ran for a then record sixty-two performances. A wittily coarse attack on the government of Whig minister Robert Walpole, it appealed to audiences for its humorous situations as well as its social satire and enjoyed a posthumous run in the twentieth century, when it was transformed by Bertolt Brecht and Kurt Weill into *The Threepenny Opera.*

Gay, who was known to his friends Jonathan Swift and Alexander Pope as "Honest" John, put his trust in financial sharks with far less probity and was nearly ruined in an overseas investment scam. Whether through bitterness over this episode or his customary joviality, he once wrote Pope that he would like the following epitaph:

Life is a jest, and all things show it.
I thought so once, and now I know it.

Pope obliged and had the couplet etched into Gay's tomb in Westminster Abbey, where he rests next to another "jester," Geoffrey Chaucer.

THE BEST TEACHER?

Sanguine wisdom suggests that experience is the best teacher and that, correlatively, we learn from our mistakes. The American writer Henry Brooks Adams articulated this belief well when he called experience an "arch, to build upon." This is a particularly popular notion with parents, who need the spur of "You'll see when you get older" to keep their children from considering them dunces.

A more pessimistic school of thought says that experience doesn't teach us anything worthwhile, because by the time we've learned something from a mistake, it's too late to do anything about it, and the lesson is unlikely to provide us guidance in future, unrelated endeavors. It's all very well, for example, to learn that speculation in penny stocks can bankrupt you. But what if your next investment opportunity is in sowbelly futures? Is the "once-burnt" lesson applicable, or irrelevant?

Whichever general attitude toward experience is "right," it seems clear that the jaundiced have the best lines. I especially like Samuel Taylor Coleridge's metaphor, expressed in his 1835 *Table Talk:* **"Experience is like the stern lights of a ship, which illuminate only the track it has passed."** Equally provocative are the Chinese proverb **"Experience is a comb that nature gives us when we are bald"** and the Pennsylvania Dutch aphorism **"Ve grow too soon olt und too late schmart."** Perhaps best—or at least most wittily resigned—is the quip from the old duffer who has been asked what he'd do differently if he had his life to live over. **"I'd make the same mistakes. Only faster."**

. . .

HERO TODAY, GOON TOMORROW

In the musical drama *Fame,* young aspirants to the mantle of Marilyn Monroe, Judy Garland, and/or Elvis Presley sing exultantly of living forever, in fine, leaping-with-the-rainbow types of lines, perfectly suited to the hopes of talented tots, but as philosophers have been telling us since the beginning of history, the desire for recognition is among the most pointless of dreams. Not only are the odds terrible, even for the supremely gifted, but getting there often brings its own disasters.

Among the famous people who have told us down the years that the view from the top ain't so hot, we might begin with the ancient philosopher Publilius Syrus, who in the first century B.C commented on celebrity loneliness: **"If you want to be known by everybody,"** he wrote in his collection *Moral Sayings,* **"then you know nobody."** The American poet Emily Dickinson, who successfully shunned recognition her entire life, snapped amusingly,

> **How dreary to be Somebody**
> **How public, like a Frog**
> **To tell your name the livelong June**
> **To an admiring Bog.**

CHAFING AT THE BIT

The German philosopher Immanuel Kant once observed that freedom is the recognition of necessity. That hard truth sat poorly with 1960s radicals, who rightly divined that such philosophical resignation might buttress a political conservatism that promoted necessity for the many, freedom for the few. But Kant's point was broader than one generation's turf battles. The fact that self-serving conservatives sometimes twist his point into a defense of backwardness does not undermine its fundamental wisdom. Denying the inevitability of this or that particular restraint is, in a democratic society, the meat of politics; denying the principle of restraint itself is a praise of bubbles.

Will Durant, the American popular scholar whose multivolume history of the world, written with his wife Ariel, has been a Book-of-the-Month Club issue for thirty years, reflected on his own experience with this tangle in a *Time* magazine story in the 1960s. Throughout his life, he said, he puzzled over the relative merits of liberty and order until he finally realized the paradoxical truth: **"Liberty is a *product* of order."** Robert Frost put it more rustically: **"You have freedom when you're easy in your harness."** The question remains, of course: Who makes the harness?

HEARING VOICES

In Freud's famous typology of mental categories, the Superego is the engine of restraint, a kind of half-internalized, half-resisted Big Brother who keeps the turmoil of the passionate Id in uneasy check. Freud himself wouldn't have said Big Brother, though. Predictably, given his obsession with early childhood, he saw the Superego as the voice of the controlling father, restricting the erotic and destructive impulses of the "child within" by imposing an irritating but socially necessary regulation. The job of this para-paternal regulator, you might say, is to make us bundles of potential anarchy afraid to misbehave.

In everyday terms, such an instillation of fear is what we call conscience, and many observers of the human psyche anticipated Freud in identifying the internalization of restraint as conscience's job. When Shakespeare's brooding Dane, for example, says **"Conscience does make cowards of us all,"** he was hinting at the mental connection between fear and probity. Oscar Wilde gives the idea a cute twist in *The Picture of Dorian Gray.* **"Conscience and cowardice are really the same things,"** he writes. **"Conscience is the trade name of the firm."**

Freud's literary contemporaries made his point more directly. The Italian dramatist Luigi Pirandello, for example, mocks conscience in *Each in His Own Way* by calling it **"nothing but other people inside you."** Somerset Maugham, sounding very Freudian indeed in *The Moon and Sixpence,* defines conscience as **"the guardian in the individual of the rules which the community has evolved for its own pro-**

tection." But the most precisely Freudian, as well as wittiest, definition comes from the Sage of Baltimore, caustic H. L. Mencken. In his 1920 *Book of Burlesques*, he calls conscience bluntly "**the inner voice which warns us that someone may be looking.**"

IT'S A BIRD, IT'S A PLANE...IT'S OVERMAN!

The German philosopher Friedrich Nietzsche is often spoken of, by those who haven't read him, as a forerunner of Nazism because he applauded the idea of an *Übermensch,* or "superman." It's claimed that the Hitlerian "super race" idea was a direct outgrowth of his thought. This would have come as quite a shock to old Fred. While he did write negatively about Jews, he also wrote negatively about practically everyone else, and was particularly contemptuous of the Germans He found anti-Semitism and "Teutonic" nationalism, which were both growing in his day, ridiculous and shameful. It was thanks partly to Nietzsche's sister, who promoted and distorted him after his death, and partly to simple sloppy reading, that we get the "superman" tossed in with the "super race."

What Nietzsche was getting at was that overcoming individual limitations—including the limitations of "accepted ideas"—is an essential part of growth and self-mastery. *Übermensch* literally means "over-man." Nietzsche's goal was to go "over" himself, that is, to work through all false doctrines and adversities so that he was constantly "remaking" himself in better form. Struggling against pain and doubt was thus essential to achieving full humanity. He put this well in *Twilight of the Idols* when he proclaimed, "**Whatever doesn't kill me, makes me stronger.**" (The Italians say the same thing in a proverb: "**What doesn't poison, fattens.**")

ONE THING

In the middle of Billy Crystal's movie *City Slickers,* a cowboy philosopher played by Jack Palance holds up a finger and says that the secret of life is "one thing." The one thing, it turns out, varies from person to person, which is not much help until you've read your own mind. But as an admonition to focus, it's well presented, and numerous Deep Thinkers have anticipated it with less economy. My two favorites are Voltaire and Thoreau.

Voltaire's version of the "one thing" philosophy comes at the end of *Candide,* where after enduring a cornucopia of misfortunes, the young hero finally achieves a revelation. Whatever life's ultimate meaning, he says, *Il faut cultiver notre jardin,* that is, **"We must cultivate our garden."** For Candide, it's a physical, squash and tomatoes garden. For the rest of us, it's whatever we "grow" best.

Thoreau's version is couched as solace to the disenchanted—those wilder spirits whose eccentric interests are not responded to by either acquaintances or the world at large. Musing on his own isolation, he comments in *Walden,* **"If one advances confidently in the direction of his dreams . . . he will meet with a success unexpected in common hours."**

HUMBLE PIE

The Germans have a concept known as *Entsagung,* or "resignation," which the more philosophical among them cite as a cure for the realization that life is too much to handle. It's not the same thing as giving up, more like a sensible, open-eyed acceptance of limitation—the kind of philosophical calm that teaches, or reflects, humility.

Scottish dramatist James M. Barrie (1860–1937), the author of *Peter Pan,* spoke well of such sobering wisdom both in *The Little Minister* and in *The Golden Book.* In *The Little Minister,* the young preacher Gavin Dishart understands that life is **"a long lesson in humility."** In *The Golden Book,* Barrie uses a professional metaphor to expand on the same notion: **"The life of every man is a diary in which he means to write one story, and writes another, and his humblest hour is when he compares the volume as it is with what he vowed to make it."**

. . .

OVER THE SHOULDER ADVICE

Leroy Robert Paige (c. 1906–1982) became one of baseball's great legends not only because of his phenomenal pitching but also because his patter was as good as his fastball. Born in Alabama, he acquired the nickname "Satchel" in the 1920s, probably because of his "satchel sized" feet, and as Satchel Paige he dominated the Negro leagues' mounds throughout the 1930s and 1940s. He was often billed as "The World's Greatest Pitcher," and the statistics do not bely the boast. Estimated to have won at least two thousand games, including about forty-five no-hitters, he was as devastating a hurler in middle age as he had been coming up. In 1933, for example, he had a 31–4 game record. Thirteen years later, he brought the Kansas City Monarchs to the Negro pennant by giving up only two runs in ninety-three innings. Among the major leaguers he faced in exhibition games during baseball's preintegrated period, he threw a 1 0 victory against Dizzy Dean and was called by ace slugger Joe DiMaggio "the best pitcher I ever faced."

After integration, Paige pitched for Cleveland and St. Louis before returning to the barnstorming circuit where he had started, sometimes sharing a mixed bill with the Harlem Globetrotters. When he was named to the American League's All-Star team in 1952, he was roughly forty-six years old. I say "roughly" because guessing Satchel's age became a popular diamond diversion, one in which he himself took considerable pleasure. When asked for the secret of his durability, he quipped, "**Avoid running at all times**" and—in the maxim that survives as his literary legacy—"**Don't look back. Something might be gaining on you.**"

NICE GUYS FINISH FOURTH

Casey Stengel and Yogi Berra both came out with so many good one-liners that they're known respectively as "Stengelisms" and "Yogi-isms." Dodger manager Leo "The Lip" Durocher seldom gets credit for more than one, but that one was a beaut. "**Nice guys finish last**" is the way it got into *Bartlett's Quotations,* although baseball experts all agree that that's misquoted. Durocher was speaking of the 1947 New York

Giants, who were having a bummer season, and what he said, motioning toward their dugout, went something like this. "**Take a look at them. All nice guys. They'll finish last. Nice guys. Finish last.**" It was only by bollixing up the inflection and fusing the last two sentences that sportswriters were able to transform this specific appraisal into a supposedly generic piece of homespun philosophy.

Not that Durocher minded. Flattered that he'd made it into *Bartlett's,* he went with the flow and called his 1975 autobiography *Nice Guys Finish Last.* The 1947 Giants, by the way, finished fourth. In the National League cellar that year were the Pittsburgh Pirates.

SPEAK TO US, O GREAT YOGI

The great Yankee catcher Yogi Berra was baseball's answer to Hollywood's Samuel Goldwyn. Like the producer, Yogi had a gift for breathing paradox into simple observations. Of a popular eating place, he remarked, "**Nobody goes there anymore; it's too crowded.**" On inflation, he mused, "**A nickel ain't worth a dime anymore.**" And when his hometown, St. Louis, threw him a party in 1947, he said gratefully, "**I want to thank everyone for making this night necessary.**"

His most famous line, though, was straight on: "**It ain't over till it's over.**" Maybe he was thinking of the impatient opera fan's classic quip "**It ain't over till the fat lady sings.**" Maybe he was merely plumbing the depths of his considerable sandlot wisdom. Whichever it was, the quote stands as his personal trademark, and as good a comment on life (or baseball) as can be found.

NEVER YOU MIND

When confronted with what the West calls the mind-body problem, Zen Buddhists tend to take an ironic—one might almost say absurdist—view. Where European philosophers spend forests full of trees and large gobbets of their own composure debating whether external reality "really" exists, the Zen master prefers to shock his or her disciple into enlightenment with the aid of puzzling koans and humorous pronouncements. Of the hundreds of koans that enliven the Zen tradition, the most famous one in the West is the unanswerable question **"What is the sound of one hand clapping?"** Of the humorous pronouncements, I especially like two from Conrad Hyers's scintillating book *Zen and the Comic Spirit*.

The first concerns the tenth-century master Fa-Yen. Pointing to a boulder, he asked a young monk whether it was inside or outside of his mind. Since "everything is an objectification of mind," said the monk, "I would have to say that the stone is inside my mind." Fa-Yen's reply: **"Your head must be very heavy."**

The second pronouncement comes from Bodhidharma, the sixth-century Indian monk who is generally considered Zen's founder. A disciple, after demonstrating his sincerity by cutting off one of his arms, begged the master, "Pacify my mind." "Bring me your mind and I will pacify it," said the master. "I have searched for it, but I cannot find it," moaned the disciple. **"There,"** said Bodhidharma, **"I have pacified your mind."**

chapter 16

The End

Death and Last Words

QUALIS ARTIFEX PEREO

Translated, this famous last word means **"Ah, what an artist is dying!"** Who would you expect to be shuffling off his or her mortal coil with that line? Picasso? Leonardo? Andy Warhol, maybe? Actually, it was the Roman emperor Nero (37–68), whom popular imagination recalls as the fellow who "fiddled" while Rome burned. History remembers him as the author of the first Christian persecutions, although he thought of himself primarily as an *artiste*. The violin hadn't been invented yet, so that part of the legend is false. But the emperor did sing and play (probably accompanying himself on the lyre), and on a visit to Greece in the year 67 was awarded a whole raft of performance prizes by intimidated judges.

As for the fire. There was one, in the year 64, and it wrecked Rome. Nero was away at his villa at the time, so it's unlikely he set the blaze himself, as he was accused of doing. He did use it as a pretext to slaughter Christians, whom *he* blamed for the conflagration, and to rebuild things in a shining Greek style. The Rome that we see in ruins today owes its inception to the grand designs of *artifex* Nero.

TALK ABOUT BEING KICKED UPSTAIRS ...

The Roman Emperor Vespasian (9–79) hasn't become exactly a household name among nonclassicists, although his most famous construction project in the Eternal City, the Colosseum, is seen by millions of tourists every year. He had been an able general along Rome's farflung frontier, and as Nero's successor he restored stability to an economy that Nero had left pretty much in tatters. His last words reflect the common practice of apotheosis, that is, the act of declaring the emperor divine. In spite of his general competence as head of state, Vespasian hadn't been accorded that honor in his lifetime. Hence his deathbed anticipation: *"Ut puto deus fio"* or **"I think I'm becoming a god."**

WELL DONE, THOU GOOD AND FAITHFUL SERVANT

History tells us that St. Laurence was a church official at Rome, that he managed the distribution of alms to the poor, and that he died by order of the Emperor Valerian in the year 258. That's it for hard facts. Thanks to legend and the writings of St. Ambrose, though, Laurence became one of the most revered of the early martyrs, renowned as much for his courage facing death as for his charity to the poor in his care.

It was the charity, according to legend, that actually brought him to death's door. Alerted that Laurence was distributing "riches" to the poor, the Roman prefect offered to spare his life if he would "donate" them to the government instead. Give me a few days, said Laurence, and I'll bring you the church's treasures.

The prefect obliged, and three days later the saint showed up with a crowd of the lame, the blind, lepers, widows, and orphans; these, he said, were the true "treasure" of the church. The prefect responded by having him broiled alive.

This might have knocked the spit out of a lesser man, but Laurence embraced his torture gleefully. So confident was he that he would soon meet God face-to-face that his last words made a joke of his agony.

"Turn me over. I'm done on this side." And, having been turned, **"I'm cooked enough. You can eat now."**

BOHEMIA FOREVER

In the fifteenth century, presaging the wars that would be generated by the Protestant Reformation, Czech nationalists intent on purifying the Catholic church resisted the hegemony of the Holy Roman Empire in a series of conflicts that became known as the Hussite Wars. Named for the reformer Jan Hus (1372–1415), who had been executed by the emperor Sigismund, the Hussites preached simplicity and poverty as well as opposition to German Catholic authority. Their first great leader, Jan Zizka (d. 1424) bested Sigismund in battles and by the summer of 1424 was in control of the country.

The power base of the most radical Hussites, the Taborites, was in Bohemia, and they are often referred to as the Bohemian Brethren. Zizka had refused to serve under Sigismund as the region's viceroy, and he remained committed to its independence until his death. That came from plague, in the fall of 1424. When he was near death, he exhorted his followers to keep up the fight in a highly unusual organ-donation statement: **"Make my skin into drumheads for the Bohemian cause."** There's no evidence that they followed his advice. The Hussite Wars ended a decade later, and the Taborites dispersed. The remaining Brethren gradually evolved into the Moravian Church.

A LITTLE GALLOWS HUMOR

Thomas More (1478–1535), author of *Utopia* and Henry VIII's nettlesome lord chancellor, died with as much dignity as he had lived. With the Reformation in full swing during his lifetime, he was faced with the same choice as every other European—whether to "protest" church abuses with Martin Luther or remain loyal to Rome. He chose the latter course, which was a problem because his sovereign had chosen the former. That More would not approve Henry's divorcing Catherine of Aragon was bad enough; but when he refused to ac-knowledge him as head of the Church of England, the rift between the two men became unbridgeable, and More was imprisoned in the Tower of London in 1534. A year later, convicted of treason on trumped-up testimony, he paid the ultimate price for his Catholicism on the headsman's block.

He went out with flair. In the Tower, he mocked the futility of Henry's power by asking, "**Is not this house as nigh heaven as my own?**" On mounting the scaffold, he spoke kindly to the lieutenant in charge, displaying again where his priorities lay: "**See me safe up, and for my coming down I will shift for myself.**" Finally, as he lay his head on the block, he first drew his beard to one side, explaining, "**This hath not offended the king.**" More was proclaimed a saint in 1935, four hundred years after his execution. If they gave points for good humor, it would have been sooner.

A SOLID ABODE

Sir John Vanbrugh (1664–1726) distinguished himself first as a dramatist, then went on to become a notable architect, producing in his masterpiece, Blenheim Palace (Winston Churchill's childhood home), a structure that has been called the culmination of the English Baroque. His comedies of manners, characterized by the typically risqué wittiness of the Restoration, included *The Relapse; or Virtue in Danger* (1696), *The Provok'd Wife* (1697), and *The Confederacy* (1705). The second of these got him accused of immorality, but without any appreciable dinting of his high spirits. In 1702 he found his second career, working with established architect Nicholas Hawksmoor on the Earl of Carlisle's country home, Castle Howard. He continued such work for the next twenty years, serving as Comptroller of His Majesty's Works throughout that period and producing, in addition to the private commissions, the Great Hall of the Greenwich Royal Hospital.

Vanbrugh's designs merged Elizabethan, classical, and Gothic features into agreeable wholes with, however, a massive quality that led his critics to call his style a "heavy" one. Among those critics, Abel Evans (1679–1737) got in the best dig. A clever-tongued cleric who was acknowledged in Pope's *Dunciad* alongside Swift, Evans had a reputation as a sound preacher but a greater one as an Oxford wit. He is the most

likely author of the brittle epitaph that made the rounds of London
society at Vanbrugh's death:

> **Lie heavy on him, Earth, for he**
> **Laid many a heavy load on thee.**

THE BEST LACK ALL CONVICTION

The best always know they could have done better. Witness one
of the most accomplished Japanese artists, Hokusai, and probably *the*
most accomplished of Western artists, Leonardo da Vinci, as just two
examples. The Japanese master, creator of the famous *Thirty-Six Views of
Mt. Fuji,* died in 1849 at the age of eighty-nine, saying, **"If heaven had
only granted me five more years, I could have become a real
painter."** Three centuries before that, surrounded by admirers at his
home in France, the greatest *uomo universale* of the Renaissance expired
at the age of sixty-seven. His biographer Vasari started a legend, since
discredited, that he died in the arms of the French king, apologizing
for his shortcomings. Whatever the tableau, his supposed last words
were a fitting testimony to his humility. **"I have offended God and
mankind,"** he said, **"because my work did not reach the quality
it should have done."**

NO EXTRA CHARGE FOR A SECOND OPINION

Of last lines most suitable to their subjects, it's hard to beat that
of the English surgeon Joseph Henry Green (1791–1863). Poetical types
know him as the devoted student and literary executor of Samuel Taylor
Coleridge, but as you might suspect, that kind of discipleship didn't pay
the water bill, so it's fortunate Green also practiced his craft of medicine.
Setting up as a surgeon in 1815, he taught anatomy at the College of
Surgeons and in various hospitals, enjoyed a solid reputation in the
operating room, and wrote frequently for both artistic and professional
journals. When this engaging fusion of the two cultures died, he provided

ex officio (and, one supposes, unpaid) assistance to the attending physician. As the doctor approached to see how he was doing, Green felt his own pulse, announced "**Stopped,**" and quit breathing.

THREE 'S THE HARM

When Union general John Sedgwick was killed at the battle of Spotsylvania in 1864, Ulysses Grant was so shocked he couldn't believe it. Twice he asked those who brought him the news, "Is he really dead?" Sedgwick, a career soldier from Connecticut, had graduated from West Point in 1837, served in the Mexican War and the Indian wars in the 1850s, and by 1864 had spent three years with the Army of the Potomac. Wounded first in the Peninsular campaign and later at Antietam, he also led his troops with consummate skill at the Wilderness and Gettysburg. Losing him, Grant commented, was like losing a division.

His death displayed both the characteristic affability that caused his men to nickname him "Uncle John" and a quite uncharacteristic lapse of judgment. His line was dug in a considerable distance from the Rebel entrenchments—too far for serious engagement but close enough for his men to be harassed by enemy snipers. Walking up to an artillery emplacement, the general compared notes with the battery commander and joked with the gunners, who were getting skittish about the seemingly random but constant firing. Don't sweat the sharpshooters, he told them. "**They couldn't hit an elephant at this distance.**" These were the last words anyone remembered him saying. A minute later, he was shot through the head.

The cuter quote books give the line as "at this dist—" but no reliable source says he was shot in midsentence. Statues of him were erected at West Point and at Gettysburg.

PÈRE-LACHAISE SECT. 17, ROW 7, GRAVE 11

The more lackadaisical quote-mongers give Oscar Wilde's dying words as "**I am dying, as I have lived, beyond my means**" or "**Either this wallpaper goes or I do.**" The Irish writer did say something similar to both these lines as he succumbed to meningitis in

Paris, but neither one was his final comment, and neither was as polished as these nuggets. According to his meticulous biographer Richard Ellman, the impoverished Wilde told a friend "I am dying beyond my means" on October 16, 1900—a painful month and a half before he died. Two weeks later, with a month of suffering and opium still ahead of him, he told another friend, "My wallpaper and I are fighting a duel to the death. One or the other of us has to go."

In November, although he chatted intermittently with visitors, Wilde became progressively incoherent. He spoke of his children, complained of mustard plasters on his feet, rambled in English and French, told friends he dreamed he was "supping with the dead," and accepted a priest's absolution. If he left any other last-hour gems, Ellmann does not record them. In what would seem to have been his last conversation, he praised *Senator North,* written by the American novelist Gertrude Atherton, and asked, **"What else has the lady written?"**

DO NOT GO GENTLE

Given the high incidence of mortality among the recently retired, there's good reason to assume that continuous activity may have something to do with the prolongation of life. That's not exactly what Dylan Thomas was getting at when he counseled the aged, **"Do not go gentle into that good night/Rage, rage against the dying of the light."** But it comes to much the same thing. Thomas and the geriatric specialist might well agree that a "relaxed old age" looks good on paper, but not in fact. Like sharks, we either keep moving, or stop moving entirely.

Essayist Frank Moore Colby made the same point about mental activity. **"Every man ought to be inquisitive through every hour of his great adventure down to the day when he shall no longer cast a shadow in the sun. For if he dies without a question in his heart, what excuse is there for his continuance?"** The seventeenth-century English bishop Richard Cumberland put it pithier, and with a predictably pious cast. Speaking of the need continually to reassess one's relationship to the Almighty, even up to the day of one's death, he said, **"It is better to wear out than to rust out."**

GOOD NIGHT, SWEET PRINCE

The most famous member of a celebrated American acting family, John Barrymore (1882–1942) was blessed with a mellifluous voice, a profile so conventionally perfect it was called the Great Profile, and enough talent to make him a star of both stage and screen. His Hamlet ranks among the half dozen or so greatest treatments of all time, while his memorable screen roles included that of the title character in the 1920 classic *Dr. Jekyll and Mr. Hyde* (he did the "change" scenes without makeup) and that of Garbo's roguish lover in *Grand Hotel* (1932). Barrymore was also afflicted, however, with a self-destructive recklessness, which led him into four marriages, countless perfunctory affairs, and the alcoholism that undoubtedly hastened his death.

His yen for the ladies is recalled in a notorious quip to ingenue Katharine Hepburn, his costar in 1932's *A Bill of Divorcement*. Irritated throughout the filming by Barrymore's none too subtle lasciviousness, Hepburn told him haughtily at the end that she would never act another scene with him. **"Really, my dear?"** the great man is reputed to have said. **"I didn't know you ever had."**

His last words also displayed a sexual preoccupation, as well as the gift for taking things lightly that charmed his friends. One of them, Gene Fowler, was with him at the end. In his affectionate biography *Good Night, Sweet Prince* (1942), he says that Barrymore, about to go, beckoned him close, wanting to whisper something of importance into his ear. Obligingly, Fowler leaned down, and heard, **"Tell me, Gene. Is it true that you're the illegitimate son of Buffalo Bill?"**

EXIT WINKING

Gertrude Stein's twin gifts to popular phraseology are her much quoted tautology **"A rose is a rose is a rose"** and her comment to Ernest Hemingway about the young people who survived World War I: **"You are all a lost generation."** The first line is immortal but vacuous and the second is second-hand (GS heard it from a French garage owner). Since I think she deserves a better legacy, let me offer the last words she ever spoke—a crisp miniplay of resignation and wan wit.

Dying of cancer in 1946, Stein was attended by her longtime companion, Alice B. Toklas, who inspired GS's "autobiography" of her and gave us hash brownies. Near the end, she looked up and asked, like any honestly confused nongenius would, **"What is the answer?"** Alice, overcome with grief, could not respond. After a moment of silence, Stein spoke again. **"In that case, what is the question?"**

NOT WITH A WHIMPER BUT A BANG

If the 1920s were the heyday of gangsterism in the United States, the movie industry caught the bug a decade later, producing a string of dark examinations of underworld types that made the "gangster movie" just as stirring an American genre as the Western or the "all-singing, all-dancing" musical. Jimmy Cagney made his mark in all three genres, but in the gangster movie he established his reputation. Only Humphrey Bogart and Edward G. Robinson were more firmly linked in the public mind during the Depression with the nightmarish excesses of the urban shoot 'em up.

The Hays Office during that period had strong feelings about how "bad guys" ought to end up on the screen, and Cagney's three most famous gangster roles all have him getting his just desserts at the close. In *The Public Enemy* (1931), he's dropped, trussed up and dying, on his mother's doorstep. In *Angels with Dirty Faces* (1938), he goes to the chair, putting on a last-minute show of trepidation to disillusion the young hoods who worship him. In *White Heat,* a 1949 late entry into the list of classic gangster portrayals, his Cody Jarrett is a psychopathic mama's boy whose violent end comes on top of a gas tank. Promising his mother throughout the film that he will one day make it to the top, he is cornered by police in a gas storage facility, climbs up the side of a tank, and is blown up when he wildly shoots the container. His last words are the film's most famous line: **"Made it, Ma! Top of the world!"**

MOTHER GODDAMN REFLECTS

Bette Davis acquired a tough cookie reputation as a Warners contract player in the 1930s, when after winning her first Oscar for the tearjerker *Dangerous,* she started refusing roles she thought unworthy of her talents. You didn't do that to Warners, or any other studio, in those days, and a juicy court battle ensued. Warners won but, chastened by the experience, started throwing the dog roles to their other starlets. Davis rewarded them with a second Oscar, for *Jezebel.*

The best comment on Davis's irascibility, and the most revealing, came from Davis herself. Around the time she got the Academy of Motion Picture Arts and Sciences' life achievement award, she sailed in, all harridan regal, to a TV talk show. Chain smoking and spluttering wisecracks, she gave a crusty reprise of her most famous movie line, **"What a dump!"** Then the host—I think it was Cavett—asked her bluntly, "How would you like to be remembered?" For her epitaph, she said, she'd like it without water. Straight and cold: **"She did it the hard way."**

THANKS FOR NOTHING

Many old headstone inscriptions are intentionally humorous, such as those that pun on the name of the deceased: a person named Young, for example, who "died Young" at the age of ninety-seven. In others, the humor seems unintentional, the sport of a writer whose heart was better than his ear. The compiler of the *Oxford Book of Death,* D. J. Enright, gives two examples from the British Isles.

In the first, a Biblical quotation that was meant to apply to the deceased reads as if it refers to the man whose poor aim did him in.

Sacred to the Memory of
Captain Anthony Wedgwood
Accidentally Shot by His Gamekeeper
Whilst Out Shooting
"Well Done Thou Good and Faithful Servant"

The second example is a grammarian's object lesson. We're all taught in the lower grades that we should place modifiers as close as possible to the words they modify. In this Edinburgh inscription, the prepositional phrase following *by* is supposed to modify the verb *erected*. Misplacing it gives the following howler:

Erected to the Memory

of

John McFarlane

Drown'd in the Water of Leith

By a Few Affectionate Friends

WHEN ANIMALS CROAK

If animals breathed "last words," what would they be? Not one of the twenty (or 120) pressing questions of all time, but interesting enough to set G. W. Stonier to thinking. An Australian-born journalist and playwright, he provided several zoological eavesdroppings, as clever as they are characteristic of their authors, which are recorded in D. J. Enright's *Oxford Book of Death*.

An expiring bird of paradise, Stonier suggests, might be tempted to exclaim, "**Home at last!**" An electric eel might mutter, "**I must tell Faraday we got there first.**" For a stallion, the lubricious meteorological pun, "**There will be mare's tails in heaven.**" For a swan, the plaintive cry, "**Leda, where are you?**" A lemming could display its alleged dimness by sighing the Greek word for *ocean:* "**Thalassa!**" A crocodile could request of the mourners, "**No tears, if you please.**" And the last dodo could simply say, "**Now I'm extinct.**"

Born in Sydney in 1903, Stonier worked for British papers and magazines throughout the 1930s and 1940s, as well as publishing at least two books that reflect an apparent ongoing fascination with animals: *My Dear Bunny* (1946) and *Round London with the Unicorn* (1951). He also wrote a war memoir with the wonderfully whimsical title *Shaving Through the Blitz* (1943).

THE GRAND PERHAPS

Nobody knows for *sure* what happens after death. The religious may be forceful and convincing in celebrating the afterlife, but they, like everyone else, are only guessing. (That's why they call it Faith.) If you *knew* what lay beyond the veil with the same clarity as you know, say, the amount of a parking fine or the color of asparagus, then you wouldn't need Faith—you'd be as smart as God.

TV evangelists today sometimes give the impression that they *are* as smart as God—that is, that they know the celestial neighborhood just as intimately as He does. The faithful of previous centuries seldom made that prideful error. François Rabelais, the lusty monk who gave us *Gargantua and Pantagruel,* was as strong a believer in the Christian afterlife as anyone of his time, but he had the humility not to second-guess the Almighty's designs. As he lay dying, painfully aware that his fate was uncertain, he murmured, "**Now I go to seek a great perhaps.**" His *grand peut-être* has been frequently echoed by later thinkers, among them the author of *Leviathan,* Thomas Hobbes, and the great nineteenth-century American preacher, Henry Ward Beecher.

Hobbes went out in 1679 with the curtain line "**I am taking a fearful leap in the dark.**" Since his writings had often displayed an anticlerical bias, he may have been registering fear of reprisal as much as ignorance. But the charge of anticlericism would hardly have stuck to Beecher. The son of evangelist Lyman Beecher and the brother of author Harriet Beecher Stowe, he was among the most widely followed Bible quoters of his time as well as a principal voice in the fight against slavery. Perhaps it was a brush with adultery charges at the age of sixty that gave him misgivings, fifteen years later, about his soul. When he died in 1887, pushing seventy-five, his last words were this prayer: "**Now comes the mystery.**"

LAST LIGHTS

As human beings close their eyes for the last time, they often refer to the encroaching darkness: Seeing a light, or asking for one, is a common theme. German writer Johann Wolfgang Goethe (1749–1832), for example, went out muttering, **"Light, more light"**—a fitting farewell for this child of the Enlightenment who had brought so much clarity and breadth of vision to his nation's literature. More sadly, the American writer O. Henry (1862–1910) left an unhappy life quoting a popular song of the time: **"Turn up the lights. I don't want to go home in the dark."** Most poetical about it was the British painter J. M. W. Turner (1775–1851), in a last line that was perfectly suited to his genius. Turner explored outdoor light more subtly than any other painter prior to the Impressionists. As his eyes closed, he whispered, **"The sun is God."**

That's all, folks.

—*Porky Pig*